DRIVING HOLIDAYS

IN THE HIMALAYAS

Uttarakhand

*"Climb the mountains and get their good tidings....
The winds will blow their own freshness into you,
and the storms their energy, while cares will drop off
like autumn leaves".*

JOHN MUIR

Author
Koko Singh

Editor
Annu Sharma

RUPA

ACKNOWLEDGEMENTS
We would like to thank Krishnan Kutty for helping us in more ways than one – leading us "off the beaten track", contributing the section on trekking and providing us infrastructural support in Ranikhet. Many thanks also to Akshay Shah for additional photographs and his help and suggestions for this edition.

First published in 2006 by
Rupa Publications India Pvt. Ltd.
7/16, Ansari Road, Daryaganj
New Delhi 110002

Sales centres:
Allahabad Bengaluru Chennai
Hyderabad Jaipur Kathmandu
Kolkata Mumbai

ISBN: 978–81–291–1152–4

10 9 8 7 6 5 4 3

Man Mohan Singh asserts the moral right to be identified as the author of this work.

Design and pre–press:
Great Latitude, New Delhi, India
www.greatlatitude.com

Cover: Flowering buckwheat in the Darma Valley

Printed in India by
Gopsons Papers Ltd
A–2&3, Sector 64, Noida 201301

Contents

A Kumaoni village home in the
Darma Valley with traditional
'likhai' wood carving

DRIVING Holidays in the Himalayas is a series of books that endeavour to give the reader a glimpse of many exciting, exotic locales that can be easily accessed by road and hopes to provide enough insight to make your holiday a comfortable and memorable one.

This book explores Uttarakhand, while the others take you through Ladakh, Zanskar, Himachal & Sikkim.

These books especially focus on travellers who are fond of driving, have their own wheels (two, four – or even hired will do!), and love the mountains. Given the time constraints of our lives today, each book is designed to cover a fair degree of terrain in a week to ten days. Although it does not aim to visit every place possible in a region, it certainly traverses a reasonable cross-section. It reflects the author's own preferences of picturesque places to visit and also makes dining recommendations ■

THE HIMALAYAS

THROUGH the ages, the Himalayas have been revered by millions of Indians as the abode of the Gods. The early 'rishis' (sages), referred to them as "the expanse of the two arms of the Supreme Being", suggestive of the whole world being locked in the Himalayas' divine embrace.

Writing in the fifth century AD Kalidas, the renowned poet, has an evocative but apt description–

In the Northern quarter is divine Himalayas,
  the lord of the Mountains,
  reaching from Eastern to Western Ocean,
  firm as a rod to measure the earth....
  There demigods rest in the shade of clouds,
  which spread like a girdle below the peaks but when the rains disturb them,
  they fly to sunlit summits....

It is here that Shiva, the great god of destruction, found solace after the death of his consort Sati, and atoned for almost destroying the world with his dance, the 'Tandava Nritya'. After wooing the bereaved Shiva for over a thousand years Parvati, the daughter of the mountains, succeeded in winning his love. The Himalayas are studded with temples dedicated to Shiva and Parvati, and every year devotees in untold numbers travel hundreds, if not thousands, of kilometers, to visit their 'abode'.

In the words of the *Skanda Purana*:
"As the sun dries the morning dew, so are the sins of man dissipated at the sight of the Himalaya".

Centuries of pilgrimage led to the building of numerous temples and hermitages, but not a single 'hill station' as we know it.

In earlier times, the local inhabitants were unaffected as the transient pilgrims were extremely limited in number due to the difficulties and time required for the arduous journey.

The first planned hill retreats were set up by the great Mughal emperors Akbar, Shah Jehan, and Jehangir who established summer palaces around Srinagar in the state of Jammu & Kashmir. The beautiful Nishat and Shalimar gardens are testament to those early endeavours and are a star attraction even today. The Mughals faded into oblivion and were followed by the British, a unique creature, unlike any other who ruled the subcontinent. They made little effort to absorb or integrate with the ancient cultures and traditions they found in this land and instead sought to create small, very British 'islands' of comfort wherever they were based. They were masters at the game of intrigue and

Mt. Kanchendzonga seen from Gangtok

treachery, playing one powerful local ruler against the other to extend and consolidate their grip over the country. However, one enemy continued to challenge – the climate.

One of the main problems faced by the British was keeping the army of almost 100,000 troops healthy. Soldiers garrisoned in the hill forts were found to be much better off

The ancient rock temple complex at Masrur, near Kangra in Himachal

capital of Himachal Pradesh) and over the next seventy years, around eighty hill stations were developed all over the country. Situated on hill tops and often even in places without a local populace, the Raj used the ample resources at its command to construct roads and railways under the most challenging conditions – who else could build railway lines to remote Darjeeling and Shimla! To give them due kudos, it is thanks to their eccentricities and desire to create conditions akin to those 'back home', far from the enervating heat, that such an extensive network of roads developed, allowing us our much-coveted driving holidays in the Himalayas.

Geologically speaking, the Himalayas are the youngest mountain range in the world and are actually still growing – up to 0.8cm annually. Samples extracted from the slopes of Mt. Everest confirm that in the past millennia, what is today the world's highest and longest (East to West) mountain range was once part of a vast ocean bed!

Eighty million years ago, in the period when dinosaurs roamed the earth – the Jurassic Age – the earth's land mass split into two great continents, Laurasia in the northern hemisphere and Gondwanaland in the southern hemisphere. Later the land mass that

than their comrades in the plains and this started the search for resorts to be used as sanatoriums.

In 1819, the first 'hill station' was established at Shimla (now the

is the Indian subcontinent broke away from Gondwanaland and floated across the Earth's surface till it ran into Asia! The collision between the hard volcanic rock of India and Asia's soft sedimentary crust resulted in the creation of all the Asian mountain ranges such as the Karakoram, Hindu Kush, Pamir, as also the Tien Shan and Kun Lun. This process took between five and seven million years and the fact that the Himalayas are at the front of the continental collision accounts for their dwarfing the other ranges and for their continued upward movement.

The Himalayas stretch 2500km from Nanga Parbat in the West (in Pakistan), to Namche Barwa (Arunachal Pradesh), in the East. The range boasts of fourteen peaks in excess of 26,200ft/8000m, including Mt. Everest, which at 29,028ft/8848m is the highest mountain in the world. The highest peak in our country is the third highest in the world – mighty Kanchendzonga (28,160ft/8585m), located in our second smallest state, Sikkim.

The Himalayan range is actually three almost parallel mountain systems. At the top lies the Great Himalayan Range with perennial snow peaks rising to heights in excess of 16,500ft/5000m, preceded by the Middle Himalayan Range of

peaks averaging between 13,000-16,500ft/4000-5000m. The foothills, or the Lower Himalayan Range, are the ranges bordering the plains with mountains around 8000ft/2500m in height and, regrettably, it is only in

this third and lowest layer of mountains that most of our driving journeys are confined!

The Himalayas are also the source of the three major river systems of the subcontinent — the Indus, the Ganga, and the Brahmaputra. All these originate from glaciers, one of which, Gaumukh — the source of the holy Ganga — is only a few kilometers from the road-head at Gangotri in Uttarakhand ■

GEOGRAPHY AND LOCATION

UTTARAKHAND was carved out of the mammoth state of Uttar Pradesh in the year 2000. It forms the northern border of India with Tibet; on the eastern side is separated from Nepal by the Kali River; has Himachal Pradesh on its West while the plains of Uttar Pradesh lie to its South.

Covering an area of approximately 51000sq km, it is larger than either Punjab or Haryana and just marginally smaller than neighbouring Himachal Pradesh. This central Himalayan belt has some of the most spectacular mountain peaks of the Indian Himalayas with over a hundred of them towering above 19,680ft/6000m. One of the better-known peaks is the Nanda Devi that lies to the East. At 25,640ft/7817m it ranks as the second highest mountain in India and twentieth in the world. It is flanked by Trishul (Shiva's allegorical trident), which stands at 23,354ft/7120m. Proceeding westwards, Dunagiri, Neelkanth, Chaukhamba and the peaks of Badrinath and Kedarnath are all in the 23,000ft/7000m league. The Gangotri and Banderpoonch peaks lie on the western extreme and below these great Himalayan peaks are the middle and lower ranges. It is here that the popular hill stations of Mussoorie, Nainital, Ranikhet and other lesser known but extremely beautiful destinations lie. The foothills are an extension of the Shivalik range that extends from Himachal Pradesh up to the Corbett National Park. Major rivers originate, join others and flow through this state. Both the Ganga and the Yamuna have their origins here and their tributaries spread through the region like a veritable network. There are five major confluences that are referred to as the 'Panch Prayag', and a pilgrimage to these is ranked a close second to visiting Sangam (at Allahabad), which is the union of the Ganga, Yamuna and the mythological Saraswati. The most important of these prayags is Devprayag where the Alaknanda and the Bhagirathi come together as the Ganga.

The Bhagirathi originates in Gaumukh above the Gangotri Temple while the merging of four other tributaries forms the Alaknanda. From East to West, the Pindar meets Alaknanda at Karanprayag, the Mandakini joins it at Rudraprayag; in the North the Dhauli Ganga merges with the Alaknanda at Vishnuprayag, near Joshimath, and the Nandakini joins it at Nandprayag. Rivers are believed to have great purifying powers and a ritual dip is akin to cleansing one's soul. The purity is meant to be more enhanced at either the source, a major confluence or at the mouth of the river ■

Traditional water mill
in Kumaon

Geography and Location

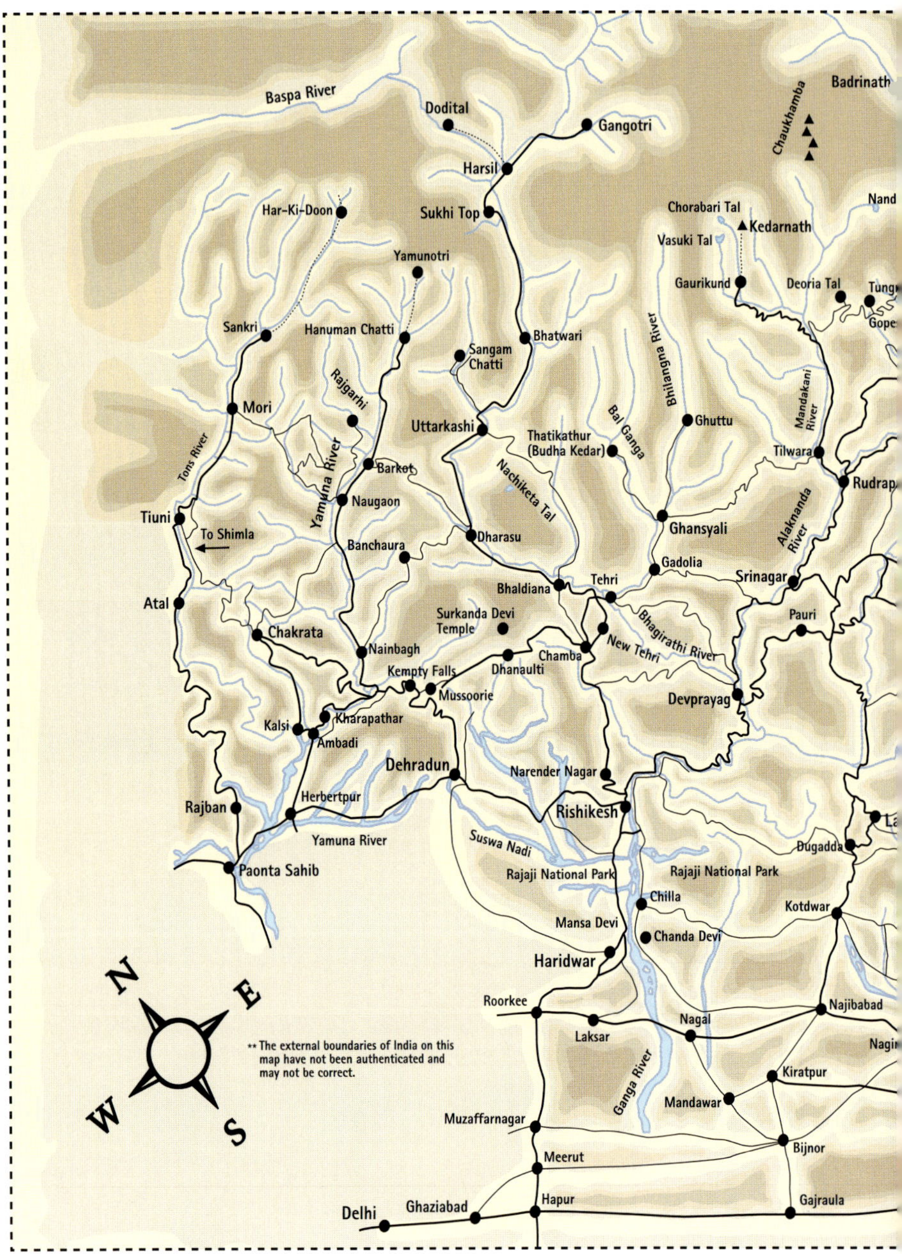

emkund Sahib
Dunagiri
Milam Glacier
▲ Nanda Devi
Pindari Glacier
Tijam
Narayan Swami Ashram
New Sobla
Munsiyari
Dharchula
Thamri Kund
▲ Trishul
Roop Kund
Nag Kund
Ghona Tal
Bendi Kund
amoli
Revati Ganga
Didihat
Thal
Ogla
Pindar River
Chaukori
Saryu River
Berinag
Ramganga River
anprayag
Gwaldam
Bageshwar
Pithoragarh
Adibadri
Gomti River
Patal Bhuvaneshwar
Baijnath
Gairsain
Ramganga River
Jageshwar
Rameshwar
Ghat
Someshwar
aurikhal
Tarag Tal
Lohaghat
Chaukhutiya
Kosi
Almora
Champawat
Baijro
Ranikhet
Manila
Khairna Bridge
Tanakpur
Kosi River
Bhimtal
Nainital
Kathgodam
Khatima
Dhangari
Haldwani
orbett National Park
Nanak Sagar
anga
oir
Ramnagar
Kaladhungi
Kashipur
Pant Nagar
erkot
Rudrapur (U.S Nagar)
ur
Ramganga River
Bilaspur
To Bareilly
Moradabad
Rampur

GETTING THERE

DELHI is perhaps the only, and certainly the easiest, gateway to Uttarakhand.

By road it is only four to six hours away from the foothills at Haldwani, Haridwar, Kotdwar and Dehradun. For those who do not want to drive in the plains, there are overnight as well as day trains to Haridwar, Haldwani and Dehradun. Visitors from the East can travel directly by train to Haldwani or Dehradun via Allahabad or Lucknow but generally speaking, most rail connections are through Delhi.

Air travellers can use the airport located between Dehradun and Rishikesh. The airport at Pant Nagar which is less than an hour out of Haldwani, is currently operational ■

PIT STOPS

There has been an exponential growth in the number of petrol pumps in the hills. As a result, it is safe to assume that there will be a petrol pump within the 100-150km range. However, it is prudent to top up whenever the opportunity presents itself as petrol supplies can be erratic in remote areas. Mechanics and tyre repair shops are to be found in most towns and the bigger towns have proper workshops. In any event, do take the precautions suggested in the section 'Driving Tips' on Page 257.

Inside the Kalika Forest

CLIMATE AND WHEN TO VISIT

THE range of Uttarakhand's terrain is such that there are extreme variations in climate; from hot summers in the Terai and lower foothills, to cold weather even during the summer months at pilgrim spots such as Badrinath and Gangotri.

The maximum summer temperature in popular hill stations such as Mussoorie, Nainital and Ranikhet generally does not exceed 32°C and

that too only when the plains are scorched with temperatures of 42°C and more. Two or three days of these heat wave conditions (by hill standards), generally result in a thunder shower, restoring the temperature to an ambient 27°C.

In winter, snowfall is common during the months December to February in most places above 6000ft/1829m. During the monsoons (July to September), rainfall is reasonably heavy and this is when landslips are most likely to occur.

You can travel around Uttarakhand throughout the year. At the height of winter Corbett Park, the Lake District (barring Nainital), as also the Rishikesh area, are very pleasant and make an ideal holiday destination. Of course, Auli is the place to go to for those looking to ski and experience the snows. The rainy season has an altogether different charm with dramatic storms and brilliant sunsets. Being enveloped by the mysterious swirling mists that rise up from the valleys is a memorable experience. Needless to say, summer is when this hill state makes an ideal escape from the enervating heat of the plains.

Uttarakhand's proximity to Delhi makes it very easily accessible and you could actually get up one morning and take off on an impromptu trip to whichever destination attracts you, at virtually any time of year ■

Agriculture and the Economy

GIVEN that Uttarakhand has a greater land mass and less than half the population of Punjab (around six million), one cannot be blamed for presuming that the people would be just as prosperous, if not more.

Sadly, nothing could be farther from the truth in this region, where over eighty percent of the people are dependant on agriculture for their livelihood. Less than fifteen percent of the land is fit for cultivation and only a single rain-fed crop is possible in most areas. Narrow valleys, dropping as sharply as 3000ft in some places, are laboriously terraced for cultivation.

Soil erosion has led to a steady deterioration in the quality of the topsoil and resulted in considerably lower yields compared to the plains. Some notable exceptions are the Dehradun valley, famed for its high quality basmati rice; the Someshwar valley in Kumaon and some parts of the Alaknanda valley in Garhwal. The plains between Rudrapur and Haldwani have well-irrigated fields with a multi-crop yield and this is a comparatively rich belt. Unlike neighbouring Himachal Pradesh, where fruit orchards (particularly apple), are a major contributor to the economy, fruit growing areas in Uttarakhand are extremely limited. Kumaon's Ramgarh area is well known for peaches, apricots and plums, while the area around Dehradun is renowned for its lichis and mangoes. However, these small oasis of rich produce do not make a major contribution to the economy, and to compound the problem, there is very little by way of food processing that could maximise benefit from the limited output. The bottom line today is that the bulk of people engaged in agriculture here can grow food to meet less than around four months of their family's annual requirement.

Another factor has been the growth of population – having been part of Uttar Pradesh for so many years, the hills did not escape the population boom. With no additional cultivable land available, the land holding per family has declined substantially and now is around 1.5 acres per family. The crops grown are coarse cereals, such as madua, barley, some wheat and in a few areas, rice and potatoes. Animal husbandry is now a major source of supplemental income but finding fodder for this burgeoning animal population is proving to be increasingly difficult. The burden falls on the women – in this case literally. It is a common sight to see women carrying a head load of almost forty kilos of leaves and grass, collected from the forest, and walking back as far as 5-8km to their homes. In fact, theirs is a very exacting day that starts before dawn

Pine resin is tapped
and collected in
conical tin containers

Women carry large heavy loads of fodder, often for long distances, to stall-feed their cattle.

– after cleaning and cooking the day's meal they head to the field or forest and return in the evening with hefty loads of fodder to complete another round of household chores.

In the sphere of industry, barring a few units in the Haridwar-Rishikesh belt, there is very little manufacturing activity worth its name. A new industrial zone has just been created outside Rudrapur but besides rewarding the industrialists with tax breaks, this is unlikely to benefit the local people to any great extent but will certainly add to traffic woes, located as it is along the highway. This somewhat bleak scenario is difficult to imagine when you are driving around the magnificent countryside. However, since agriculture and other sources of income do not provide more than six month's sustenance, the result is what is known as the 'money order economy'. The army is the largest source of jobs in this region, with at least one member of a family serving or having served in the armed forces. Since recruitment starts at the tender age of eighteen, the villages end up loosing most of their young men. Those who do not get in to the army migrate anyway; usually to become part of the service industry – mainly employed as domestic servants, waiters and cooks in eateries across the country or working as office staff.

The root of this economic malaise can be traced to the British Empire and its skewed priorities for development. Prior to their taking control of the forest, the people enjoyed a symbiotic relationship with the jungle that met their needs for fuel, fodder and construction. The British cut huge swathes of forest for the timber required to build the railway network and to construct their cantonments. The mixed forests of yore were gradually converted to pine that has greater commercial value than the broad leaf varieties such as oak. Cut off from their forests, the local populace concentrated on increasing cultivation to meet their growing needs. They cut more and more terraced fields on the hill slopes – even those not ideal for agriculture.

Unfortunately, the new 'rulers' of our country have mostly continued the same policies and one cannot help but wonder how long the colonial mindset and its attendant baggage will weigh us down. Today, more than fifty years after independence, the forest department acts as lord and master of the jungle; pine is still the preferred species and the proceeds from the resin and wood sold commercially goes to the government coffers. Shrubs do not grow under pine trees because of the acidity the soil acquires from pine needles. The people are therefore

Rich paddy fields descending to the river bed in Someshwar valley

compelled to continually lop off leaves and branches of the other varieties. There is a growing confrontation between the real owners, the people, and the controlling authority, that is in this case, the government. All is not yet lost and in a few forest ranges, pine plantations have been replaced with broad-leaf varieties. Some efforts are being made to revive the traditional Van Panchayats. However, these belated moves will have to be widespread and move with the speed of lightening to have any real impact.

Tourism is gradually emerging as a major source of revenue for the local population and possibly has the highest potential to give the local economy a boost. The government could do a lot in this sphere, not only by improving infrastructure and facilities but also by developing new, beautiful locales in an eco-friendly manner rather than allowing unfettered growth and crowding of existing hill stations ■

The Environment

THERE are serious well-founded concerns regarding reduced tree cover and the resultant soil erosion, drying up of small springs, reduced rainfall and the incidence of flash floods.

Unfortunately, on analysis, it becomes evident that a substantial part of the problem has been created by our misplaced and misguided development priorities. To cite a few examples:

The long term environmental damage caused by road building has never been evaluated. The PWD has an annual allocation of funds to spend and roads are often constructed in areas where the hillsides are so fragile that more time and money is spent on keeping the road open than was initially spent on the actual construction (Perhaps this is a good method of employment generation!). The follies at the local level are compounded at the center. The last government announced the construction of a four-lane highway to Badrinath and now the current one is set to compete with some more mindless genius – a motor road to Hemkund Sahib has been proposed! All this in a fragile eco-system....

More than enough has been written on the controversial Tehri Dam but there are numerous other projects that have been commissioned without any public debate. Besides displacement of people, these projects all involve large-scale permanent destruction of thousands of hectares of forest and you can see the scarred and ravaged hillside for miles – the drive beyond Joshimath is one such mega-eyesore. These dams also run the risk of being subject to earthquakes on a Himalayan scale since this is a seismic zone.

There is a perceptible preference now for hydel power but even these projects must undertake a detailed analysis on environmental impact – not only on fragility of the mountainside but also the balance of the eco-system; flora, fauna and impact of these changes on people's lives.

There is an urgent need to take a step back and contemplate the consequences of our actions before we bring in an 'environmental kalyug'.

Another major contributing factor is the forest management policy being followed by the state (see section on Economy). The writing on the wall is clear – almost sixty years of government control has led to a large reduction in the quality and quantity of forest. Data from the impartial National Remote Sensing Agency has shown a decline of 1.3 million hectares per annum (nationally), over a seven-year period during the late 1970s. The only reasonable alternative is handing over management of this scarce resource to those whose lives depend on it – the people.

The other dangerously scarce resource in the mountains is water and this is cause for deep concern that needs to translate into immediate, ecologically sustainable action. It is the saddest commentary of all that in this land – the birthplace of such mighty rivers – it is a common sight to see women and children hefting heavy water containers uphill from an apology for a stream. Young boys have fashioned a new kind of vehicle – a board on wheels, steered by ropes. They walk uphill to the nearest roadside hand pump and hurtle down on the board with their precious cargo of water – dangerous but expedient transportation.

It is imperative we look for long-term answers – pumping water over great distances in unsightly pipes,

Forest fires are common in summer

from depleted streams is certainly not the answer. The water sources need to be addressed — broad leaf forest cover in the catchment areas just has to be built up so that water from precipitation is caught and allowed to percolate into the ground and recharge the drying sources.

Uttarakhand has witnessed a number of people's movements on environmental issues and possibly the most famous of these is the 'Chipko Movement'. The Chipko (cling to), struggle had its genesis in the 1970s when the state government awarded contractors in Chamoli district the right to commercial felling of vast tracts of forest. This was in complete violation of Panchayat laws and the practices followed even under British rule. The people did not need to be told that this was a threat to their very existence. With wisdom passed down the generations, they understood well their relationship with the forests. Without these forests, there would be no fodder, fuel or water, leaving them with the option of either starving or permanently relocating their homes.

The burden of all forest related activities, in addition to the normal domestic chores, was borne by the women and being directly affected, they took the lead in this protest. When a group of axe wielding loggers arrived, the women formed a

More recently, in the mid '90s, the inherent environmental consciousness of local women has been tapped in a unique manner. The word 'Maiti' is derived from 'mait', the Kumaoni term for a married woman's paternal home. The strong emotional ties of parents with daughters who leave their home and village after marriage, led to the birth of a new custom — as part of the marriage ceremony, the bride and groom plant a tree. In fact, in the Pindar valley, wedding invitation cards detail the time and location of the 'maiti' plantation ceremony. This has resulted in groves of 'maiti' trees in many villages and these are looked after by the 'maiti behene' – village girls who are not yet married. Since this is a community asset, occasions other than marriage, such as birthdays, religious festivals and other local events, are used as an opportunity to add a tree to the village maiti forest. May many thousands of maiti forests bloom!

ring around the trees, hugging them to prevent the cutting. This initial resistance converted itself into a full-fledged movement in the '80s. Gaura Devi and Sudesha Ben were among the more prominent leaders.

Veiled in controversy — the Tehri Dam, now nearing completion

This unique method of clinging to protect the trees evolved from the Gandhian policy of non-violent protest.

This Chipko Movement attracted widespread attention and many others joined the fray. Ghanshyam Raturi, popularly known as Saileniji, took on the role of the ideologue and is well known for his songs based on the movement: "— *chipko yon daliyan par, avnakatan diya* —" (embrace the trees and stop them from felling).

Sunder Lal Bahuguna, a Gandhian activist and philosopher (now famous for his opposition to the Tehri Dam), also joined the movement, and the government was finally compelled to cancel the contract and impose a ban on felling. The Chipko Movement has proved to be the fountainhead for other environmental struggles such as those against indiscriminate quarrying and mining and the 'beej bachao andolan' (a campaign to preserve the genetic heritage of crops grown in the area) ■

FLORA AND FAUNA

DUE to its climatic variations and the range of natural terrain, Uttarakhand is blessed with an extremely wide variety of flora and fauna.

The region can be divided into climatic zones, starting with the sub-tropical zone that includes the terai jungle and the foothills up to an altitude of 3936ft/1200m. Teak and sal forest interspersed with katechu, haldu, toon, neem, red silk cotton and mango trees dominate lower regions of this zone. The beautiful yellow laburnum blooms in May and is preceded by the stunning mauve jacaranda that blossoms a little earlier. The dhak (coral tree) bears vivid scarlet flowers in clumps at the end of its branches (March to May); and the 'flame of the forest' (amaltas), has distinctive orange flowers that colour the landscape between February and May. Poplars, bottle brush and bamboo are commonly seen in parts of this region as also the cannabis shrub that grows wild, in ragged dusty clumps by the road side and also at higher altitudes.

Above this sub-tropical belt is the

The Himalayan fox, crossing the road near Pauri

temperate zone, extending upto the tree line, and the change in flora between the two is quite dramatic. The pine begins to dominate and there are belts of dense mixed forests of oak (banj), birch (bhoj) magnolia, mimosa, horse chestnut and silver oak. There is also a variety of fruit bearing trees like peaches, plums, apples and pears. Above 5904ft/1800m, the stately deodar makes its presence and is commonly seen up to 7872ft/2400m. The rhododendrons (buransh), can be seen in this belt and their brilliant red, and sometimes pink, flowers bloom in March-April adding vivid splashes of colour to the forests. Between 7872ft/2400m and 11,808ft/3600m, you see spruce, fir, cypress and some blue pine.

Floral species include geraniums, asters, lilies, arum, agapanthus and iris, pontentillas, roses, anemones, marigolds, orchids, tree dahlias, primulas, hydrangeas, cosmos, daisies, fritillaria, the white Columbra (koonj), lady's slipper and many many other beautiful blooms. An amazing range of medicinal plants and herbs also grow in parts of this state.

With around 7500 species of plants, the western and central Himalayas are one of the richest regions of bio diversity in the world.

Uttarakhand is a bird watcher's paradise with over 230 species in the state. You can spot babblers, thrushes, tits, magpies, bulbuls, flycatchers, warblers, finches, orioles, minivets, shrikes, nightjars, owls, pheasants, woodpeckers, pigeons and even the rarer Himalayan golden eagle, trangopan, monal and Himalayan bearded vulture. This area has amazingly vibrant and varied birdlife. The best areas to go bird watching are Naukuchiyatal, the Binsar sanctuary and the Har-ki-doon valley. Animal life also abounds but with the pressure of population, the animals can best be spotted in the protected sanctuaries and parks. Corbett National Park offers a wide spectrum of wildlife of the region in a compact space.

Uttarakhand is home to various species of deer, including the chital, barking and musk deer; wild elephant, wild boar, civet cats, porcupines, pine martens, foxes, black and brown Himalayan bear, leopard and the majestic but elusive tiger. At higher altitudes, you may come across goral, ibex, bharal and if you are really very lucky, the snow leopard, which has been seen in Auli.

Recently the uncontrolled explosion in numbers of langur and rhesus monkeys has become a major menace in hill towns – particularly at pilgrim spots and tourist haunts where they are not only demanding but also aggressive ■

HISTORY RELIGION AND PEOPLE

INSPITE of the paucity of records, scattered fragments of evidence stand testimony to the fact that this mountainous land was inhabited and civilised many thousands of years ago. Archaeological excavations have revealed implements that date back to the Stone Age (8000 BC). From the pre-Christian Era are frescoes on cave walls depicting scenes of hunting and sacrifice. There was considerable emphasis on temple building through the ages and various etchings and carvings have been found from the second century BC through to the thirteenth and fourteenth centuries. A few sixth century copper plates provided a wealth of information — like the one at Brahmpura, near Bageshwar, and the Taleshwar Copper Plate.

Uttarakhand ('Northern Land'), is historically a spiritually evocative term for Hindus who looked upon this land, from the earliest times, as home of the gods. It is a land of popular myths with history, religion

The erstwhile Maharaja's palace at Narendra Nagar, now the world famous Ananda Spa and Resort

and spiritual lore weaving together the very fabric of its society. These majestic mountains have held an eternal calling for spiritual seekers. Religion became the mainstay of all aspects of life here – from festivals to lifestyle and to the arts, as is evidenced by the prolific temple building through every age.

Given the extent and complexity of

the predominant religion, Hinduism, and the close intermingling of history and religion – or spiritual lore – in this region, the two subjects are being dealt with together.

The eleventh century Sun Temple at Katarmal

As the scriptures, the Vedas, shifted their emphasis from the Indus to the River Ganga, this land grew in spiritual significance and acquired the reverent status of 'Devbhoomi', the land of the gods. The scripture refers to 'Saptasindhu' – the land of seven rivers – as home of the Aryans, or Vedic people, and these seven rivers are those that merge to form the River Ganga in Garhwal. They are, from East to West, the Bhagirathi, Alaknanda, Pindar, Dhauli Ganga, Mandakini, Nandakini and Nayar.

With the growing influence of the Aryans and the Brahminical priests, indigenous people were given a lower social status and over a period of time society was divided along caste lines. The advent of Buddhism, around 530 BC, presented a threat to Brahminical orthodoxy, as its rejection of the caste system was appealing. During the reign of Ashoka the Great (around 260 BC), Buddhism became the state religion and spread far and wide – even across the Himalayas to Tibet. This religion continued to grow till the influence of the great Hindu reformer, Adi Shankaracharya came to prevail. This famous monist philosopher made frequent visits to the Himalayas. It was at Joshimath that he meditated before embarking on his quest for the revival of Hinduism and this place became the first of the four 'Maths' (centers of learning). The first 'Dham' (religious center), was also established at nearby Badrinath in the form of a temple dedicated to Vishnu. As he succeeded in restoring the supremacy of the Brahminical order, Buddhism receded in importance and the only remaining trace is the Ashokan rock edict at Kalsi, near Dehradun.

The expansion of the Indus Valley civilisation between 2500 – 1500 BC led to migrations and this mountainous area, particularly the foothills, came under external influence. The Kassites (Khasas or Sakas) were of Scythian origin and spread through the region now recognised as Kumaon, Garhwal, Kullu and Nepal. The Katyuri rulers of Kumaon were a Khasa tribe and the Mahabharata assigns 'the region near the source of the Yamuna and Ganga' to the Khasas.

Today Uttarakhand comprises the culturally distinct provinces of Kumaon and Garhwal but historically till the eighteenth century, these were separate kingdoms and often at loggerheads with each other. Earlier known as Kartripur, Garhwal (the place of forts), consisted of fifty-two fiefdoms, each with its fortified castle.

Son Pal was the first Raja of Garhwal about whom there exist

precise records. He was based in the Bhilangana valley and held sway over western Garhwal. Having no son, he was succeeded by his son-in-law, Kadil Pal who was from the Panwar dynasty of Dharanagar. It was Ajai Pal, a descendant of Kadil Pal, who consolidated the scattered fiefdoms of Garhwal under one authority and shifted the capital from Chandpur to Devalgarh.

Balbahadra Sah was the first king

to drop the surname 'Pal' and adopt 'Sah' which is the name still borne by the descendants of the erstwhile state of Tehri.

A descendant, Dularam Sah was the first to come in contact with the Chands of Kumaon. He fought a brief but decisive battle with Rudra Chand (1565-1597), the ruler of Kumaon at that time. However, Rudra Chand and his son Lakshmi Chand continued to battle with the

It's time for festivities!

Sahs several times with some gains and some losses. Later, Mahipati Sah shifted the capital from Devalgarh to Srinagar. During the reign of Pirthi Sah in the early seventeenth century, the Muslim rulers of Delhi invaded Garhwal and took over Dehradun but Pirthi later made peace with them. Conflict with Kumaon continued throughout with raids and counter raids into each other's territory. Pradip Sah, one of the most important rulers of Garhwal came to power in 1717, made peace with the Kumaonis and heralded a period of prosperity in both states.

This prosperity attracted the Rohillas who took over Dehradun from 1757-1770 and occupied Almora in 1745. At this point, Kalyan Chand of Kumaon appealed to Pradip Sah for help and the combined forces of Kumaon and

Meticulously maintained, the Somnath Parade Ground at Ranikhet

Garhwal came together to battle the Rohillas but suffered a humiliating defeat. Even Srinagar was threatened and a handsome sum was paid by Pradip Sah on behalf of Kalyan Chand and the Rohillas withdrew completely.

Neighbouring Kumaon had two dynasties – the Katyuris, who ruled from eighth to twelfth century and the Chands who succeeded and ruled till the eighteenth century.

The term Kumaon is believed to have originated from Kurmanchal (the 'land of Kurmavtar'), as it was believed to be the land where Lord

Vishnu adopted his tortoise 'avatar' (incarnation).

The Katyuris had their capital at Brahmpur (near Bageshwar), and it became a center of learning and the arts. A great number of temples were built during the reign of the Katyuris and the rich heritage of beautiful temple complexes at Joshimath, Baijnath, and Jageshwar is attributed to them. Their successors, the Chand dynasty, initially had their capital at Champawat but later moved it to Almora.

There are few records available of the Katyuri dynasty but apparently the last king, Vir Dev, was a despised despot who earned the hatred of his people by subjecting them to unprovoked looting and harsh taxation. At the end of their tether, an unusual solution was found – his palanquin bearers sacrificed themselves by jumping off a cliff while transporting the king, thereby releasing the people from continued exploitation!

After his death, a civil war broke out and the kingdom disintegrated till Som Chand from the Chand (lunar), dynasty of Prayag was invited to marry a Katyuri princess and rule the state. The Chand dynasty continued till the eighteenth century and was marked by relative prosperity and stability. The original capital at Champawat was shifted to Almora in the sixteenth century and the reign of Lakshmi Chand (1597-1621) is notable for two interesting anecdotes:

Due to unsustainable heavy taxation on cultivable land, people began growing vegetables on their rooftops and though taxes were finally reduced, this practice can be seen even today in some places.

Continuing the traditional rivalry with the Garhwalis, Lakshmi Chand conducted many raids on them with little impact. However, he notched a small success on his eighth foray and this news was conveyed to Almora by lighting small fires on hilltops and this occasion is celebrated so even today. Interestingly, on their side, the Garhwalis were claiming and communicating the defeat of the Kumaonis in the same way!

As you have already read, in 1745 the Rohilla army attacked, conquered and took over the Chand kingdom. Although the army indulged in widespread plunder and looting, the Jageshwar group of temples remained unscathed. Local legend has it that a vast swarm of bees descended on the Rohilla army, preventing them from approaching the temples.

Towards the end of the century, both kingdoms of Kumaon and Garhwal, which were weakened by their internecine feuds, fell prey to the Gorkha army of Nepal. Not satisfied with this success, the Nepalese forces made repeated incursions into adjoining areas that were under British control. In 1814, war broke out with the British and by 1816 the Gorkha army was defeated with the longest siege taking place at Kumpur, near Ranikhet, which lasted from February 1815 till March 1816. The British were now the masters of Kumaon and Garhwal but as an act of clemency, the Raja of Garhwal was handed over half of his former territory with the new capital being established at Tehri.

A natural corollary to the British conquest of this region was the development of hill stations, the most prominent being Mussoorie, Nainital and Ranikhet.

Under British rule, the first commissioner, G.W. Traill, established a uniform revenue tariff and set up administrative and police systems adapted to suit conditions in the hills. Subsequently, Sir Henry Ramsay settled land records and

Weather-beaten but happy!

further consolidated the British position – there was a general level of satisfaction with the 'New King'. In fact so much so that the 1857 Independence movement (which the British term the mutiny), did not spread to the hills.

However, the British were responsible for introducing two new systems that were particularly repugnant to the hill people. The first was compulsory coolie labour to assist them in their troop movements, construction of cantonments, roads etc. The exploitation was in the form of

Indian Military Academy (IMA), Dehradun

'Kulibegar' or labour 'Bardyash', which demanded that locals provide touring British officials with free food and supplies. Labour for movement of materials, supplies as also for forestry had to be provided. Although on paper this labour was to be paid for, this rule was observed largely as an exception.

The second major change was the introduction of forestry for commercial purposes and the subsequent creation of reserve areas.

This deprived the people of their traditional access and usage of fodder, fuel and timber from the forests. In 1916, Govind Ballabh Pant and other like-minded people founded the Kumaon Parishad to systematically oppose the British — people had now reached the stage when they were ripe for organised opposition and launched an agitation against the Rowlatt Act in 1919. In 1921, Badri Dutt Pandey, Govind Ballabh Pant and others subjected the various 'coolie' practices to scathing criticism at Bageshwar. Registers that contained the names of coolies were dumped in the Saryu River and from here on the people of this region became an integral part of the freedom struggle.

After India's Independence, another kind of struggle gained momentum — that for a separate independent state carved out of the huge state of Uttar

Pradesh. The rationale was the differences in culture, language, environment and traditional livelihood patterns of the people of this region versus the rest of the state. It was believed that both political and administrative power was wielded from the far away capital with practically no representation from this mountainous region. These communities felt marginalised and believed the governing authorities had little or no sensitivity to, or understanding of, conditions and problems peculiar to the hills. This distancing led to minimal employment opportunities and development programmes and did not take into account people's symbiotic relationship with Nature while formulating policies that affected their natural resources and livelihood patterns.

Uttarakhand Kranti Dal was formed in 1979 with the objective of creating a new state and the movement received further impetus in 1994 with the active support of students. They were upset over the policy of reservations as they saw themselves losing jobs to migratory 'backward classes'. Women too were an active support group – lack of employment opportunities had forced their men folk to migrate and they had borne the burden of this too long.

In 1994 matters started to precipitate; a group of agitators on a hunger strike were 'lathi-charged' in Pauri and shortly after, police fired on protestors in Mussoorie leaving two women dead. Instigated by these events, all political parties came together under a Joint Struggle Committee and agreed to demonstrate in protest before the Parliament. Protestors were moving

Remnants of history — an abandoned British cemetery just out of Nainital

in large numbers to Delhi when the police intercepted them at Muzaffarnagar. In the ensuing confrontation people were killed and women raped. These atrocious incidents mounted huge pressure on the administration and in political circles. The struggle continued with a single-mindedness that finally yielded rewards – Uttaranchal (now renamed Uttarakhand in late 2006), a separate state, came into existence in November 2000.

This region's very identity is inextricably linked with its numerous religious shrines – ardent Hindus dream of making a pilgrimage at least once in their lifetime to this abode of their Gods. The Char Dham (four sacred shrines), of Gangotri, Yamunotri, Kedarnath and Badrinath are in Garhwal and Haridwar, as the name suggests, is the gateway to them. Those on a spiritual quest inevitably find their way to Rishikesh, a great pilgrimage center and the site of many an ashram with learned yogis and gurus. The entire region abounds in temples and shrines to various Gods of the Hindu pantheon – from the popular Shiva to various forms of Devi (Shakti), to Vishnu, Surya (the Sun God) and a number of powerful, highly evolved sages. There are as many lore linking them to their abode and this makes Uttarakhand a symbol of faith.

PEOPLE

Although almost entirely of the Hindu religion, there is considerable diversity within the people of the state. There are four tribal groups with a substantial presence, particularly in areas bordering Nepal and Tibet. Of these, the Bhotiyas, who are of Mongoloid origin, are found in the northern and eastern region. 'Bhot' is the Sanskrit word for Tibet and hence Bhotiya, or Bhutia, applies to those who originated from there. The Bhotiyas in Uttarakhand are divided into at least three sub-sects, all sharing a common origin but each with their own distinct language and culture. The Malla Johar Bhotiyas are in the Munsiyari region, with a large concentration in Milam.

The Marchas reside in the Vishnuganga valley while the three branches of the Dharchula Bhotiyas are spread over the Darma, Byans, Chaudas valleys.

Another group of Mongoloid origin, known as the Jadhs live in Uttarkashi district in the northwest of the state. The Yamuna valley is home to the Jaunsaris who trace their ancestry to the Pandavas.

In the Terai belt, the original inhabitants are the Buxas and the Tharus, both of whom are descendants of the Mongols of Central Asia ◼

THE HOLIDAY

ƒrom now on, the author takes the steering wheel and leads you through a most scenic and spectacular land, with an itinerary that unfolds over the next pages...

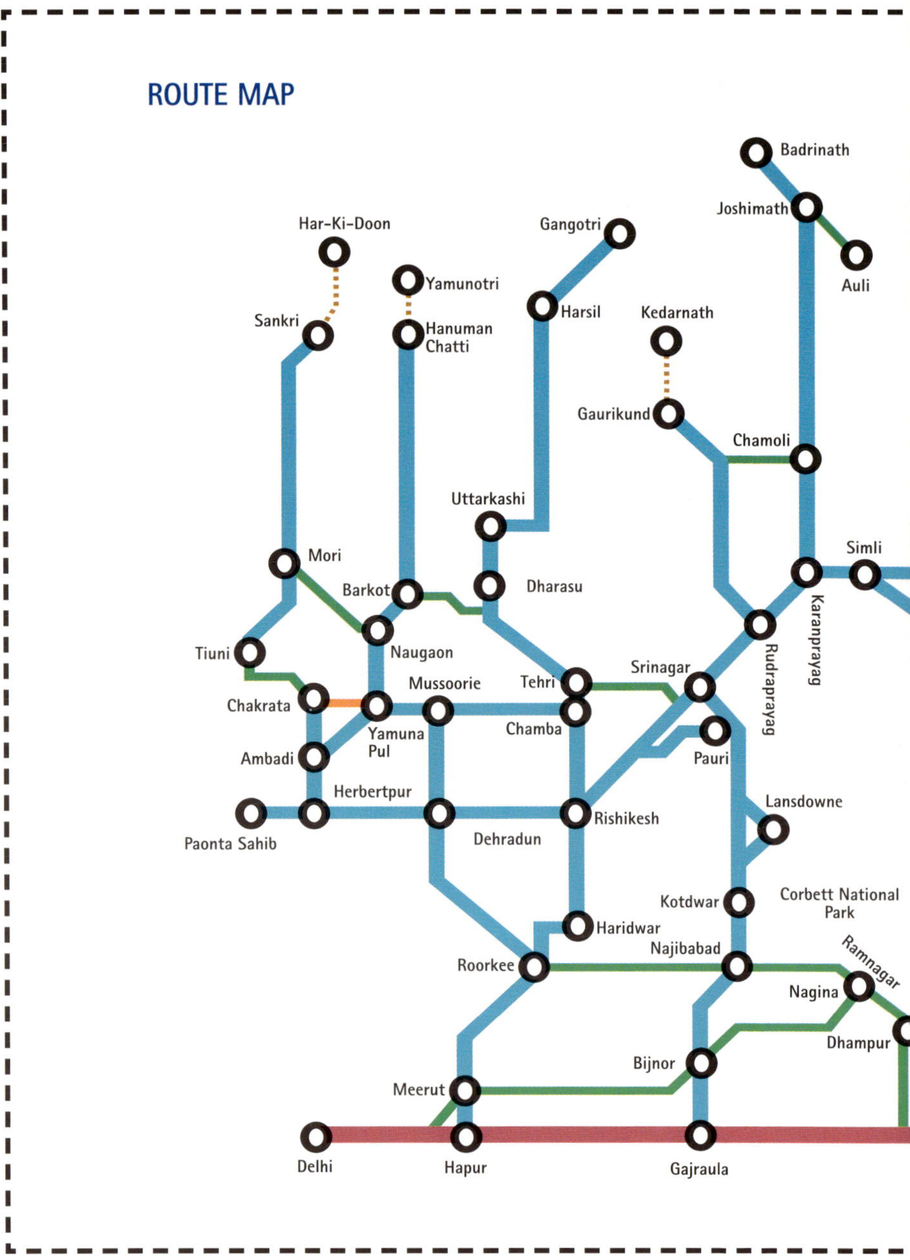

Badrinath
Joshimath
Auli
Har-Ki-Doon
Gangotri
Yamunotri
Sankri
Harsil
Kedarnath
Hanuman Chatti
Gaurikund
Chamoli
Uttarkashi
Simli
Mori
Dharasu
Barkot
Karanprayag
Tiuni
Naugaon
Rudraprayag
Chakrata
Mussoorie
Tehri
Srinagar
Ambadi
Yamuna Pul
Chamba
Pauri
Herbertpur
Lansdowne
Paonta Sahib
Dehradun
Rishikesh
Kotdwar
Corbett National Park
Haridwar
Ramnagar
Najibabad
Roorkee
Nagina
Dhampur
Bijnor
Meerut
Delhi
Hapur
Gajraula

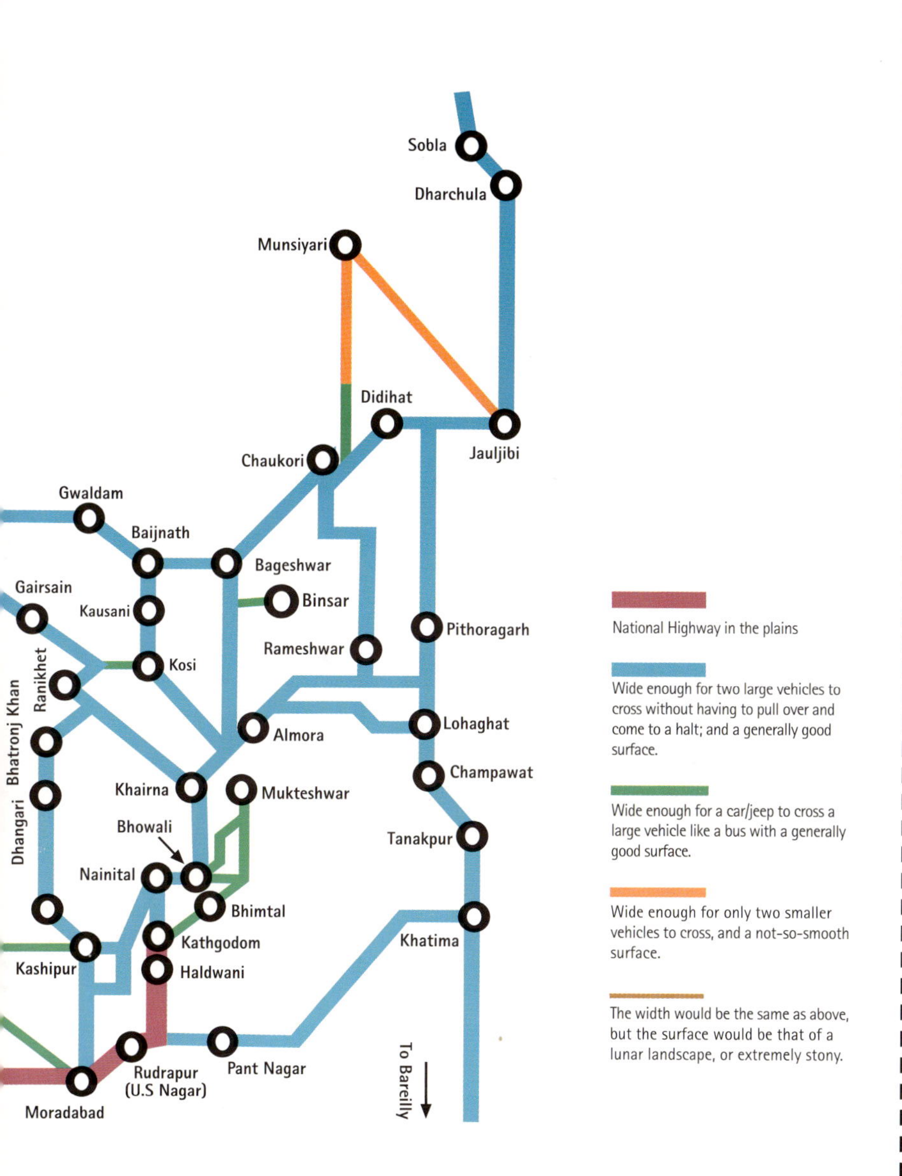

Sobla
Dharchula
Munsiyari
Didihat
Jauljibi
Chaukori
Gwaldam
Baijnath
Bageshwar
Gairsain
Kausani
Binsar
Pithoragarh
Rameshwar
Ranikhet
Bhatronj Khan
Dhangari
Kosi
Almora
Lohaghat
Khairna
Mukteshwar
Champawat
Bhowali
Tanakpur
Nainital
Bhimtal
Kathgodom
Khatima
Kashipur
Haldwani
Rudrapur
(U.S Nagar)
Pant Nagar
To Bareilly
Moradabad
National Highway in the plains
Wide enough for two large vehicles to cross without having to pull over and come to a halt; and a generally good surface.
Wide enough for a car/jeep to cross a large vehicle like a bus with a generally good surface.
Wide enough for only two smaller vehicles to cross, and a not-so-smooth surface.
The width would be the same as above, but the surface would be that of a lunar landscape, or extremely stony.

TRAVEL PLAN

THE HIMALAYAN ODYSSEY

DAY 1
▶▶ **Drive to Bhimtal or Naukuchiyatal**

Don't let the grand double lane highway fool you into complacency — you will have to dodge potholes and stray cattle soon after the Hapur bypass!

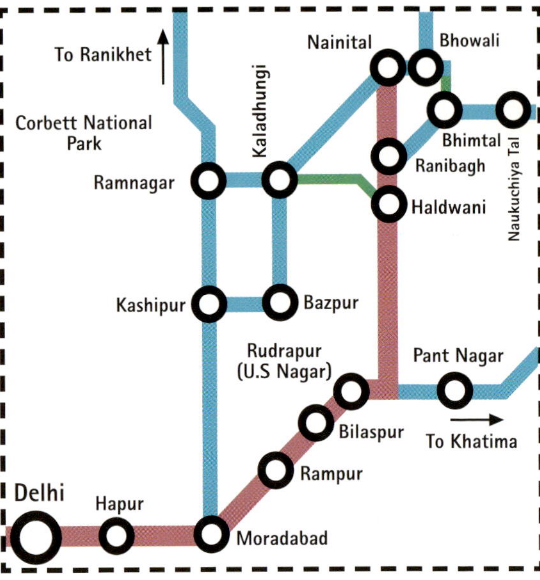

Delhi-Gajraula	105 km	Rudrapur-Kathgodam	36 km
Gajraula-Moradabad	55 km	Kathgodam-Nainital	34 km
Moradabad-Rampur	21 km	Kathgodam-Bhimtal	21 km
Rampur-Rudrapur	46 km	Bhimtal-Naukuchiyatal	6 km

An early start out of Delhi is an absolute must as you can save up to an hour by leaving before 6 a.m. and we would like to get you out of the city and into your holiday by lunch on the very first day. The road has dual carriageway only up to the end of the Hapur bypass (around 50km) and from there on even though the road surface is good you have to negotiate the usual tractor-trolleys, buses, trucks, bullock carts and cyclists weaving across the highway. One unique road hog that you will encounter on the section up to

The 'Maruta' A.P.V.
(all purpose vehicle!!)

Moradabad is 'Ulta Pradesh's' answer to Henry Ford – the 'Maruta'! Local mechanics have fashioned a vehicle run on a diesel pump and it can chug along, with a full cargo, at 15-20kmph!

En route you cross Garh Mukteshwar on the banks of the Ganga, which is being developed as a pilgrim center and bathing ghat. On festivals and other auspicious days people throng here in great numbers to take a holy dip and this

An eye-catching range of 'murhas' in all shapes and sizes sold by the road side en route to Garh Mukteshwar

sometimes leads to traffic jams.

A hundred kilometers along your journey you come to Gajraula and this can be your first pit stop – it is famous for its paranthas and these, washed down with tea, coffee or a cold glass of lassi constitute a hearty enough breakfast to set the right tone to your holiday! Barring unforeseen traffic jams it should take under two hours to reach here and there is a variety of dhabas to

Off-the-road facilities are definitely looking up. Decent toilets are available at the Reliance and HP/BP petrol pumps up till Rampur and there are plenty of repair shops.

A field of cheery sunflowers brightening the landscape near Rudrapur

choose from as well as a couple of motels and the Reliance A-1 Plaza just beyond the crowds of the main town.

After this, you drive to Moradabad, which till two years ago was infamous for its congested roads and inevitable traffic jams that could retard your progress by a couple of hours, or even more. There is now a bypass in place and the Rs. 25 toll charge is indeed a small price to pay for escaping the quagmire.

Around 8km before Moradabad there is a sign marking the bypass to the right. It is a good, fast paced road but watch out for the four bridges along this route — in just two years some sections of the road have 'sunk' almost six inches and are misaligned so if you don't watch out, these can jar the living daylights out of you!

At the end of the bypass, turn right for Rampur. For those who sped past Gajraula, you can make a pit stop at the Hindustan Petroleum Jubilee Dhaba or at another one of the swanky Reliance Pump's A-1 Plaza complexes.

There is yet another potential for delay — a railway crossing 4km before Rampur. If you do get held up, keep in mind that in season the guavas sold here are rather good and shopping for these beats fretting uselessly! Driving through Rampur town you pass a quaint and disused old railway station next to the new one, and at the blue overhead sign you turn left on NH87 towards Nainital.

Bilaspur, the next town, is 30km ahead. Negotiating through this is messy enough but the real constraint is a narrow single lane bridge just as you are pulling out of town. Impatient drivers end up causing frequent hold ups even in the normal course but if you are unlucky enough to meet heavy traffic (as we once did when the actress-cum-politician Jaya Prada came campaigning to what is now her constituency), it can be very annoying indeed! What frustrates you even more is that there are no signs of even attempting to address this simple problem.

A short drive of 15km brings you to Rudrapur (Udham Singh Nagar). You cannot help but notice the predominance of Sikhs in the Bilaspur-Rudrapur belt — they were assigned this land when the division between India and Pakistan dislocated them. This Terai belt was considered an inhospitable terrain with forests and tangled undergrowth and it took sheer toil and labour before these industrious people could convert it to

Meriton near Gajraula and Holiday Regency just short of the Moradabad bypass, are good stopping options. In the summer you can take an ice cream break at the outlet next to the petrol pump as you enter Bilaspur.

The Haldwani to Kathgodam section is like driving in Old Delhi at peak traffic! Scooters and auto rickshaws weave through with scant regard and you breathe easy only when you hit the first gentle curve past the railway station.

the lush fields we drive through today. A bountiful crop of wheat, corn, rice and mustard is grown here and in recent years you see an increasing number of fields of beautiful sunflowers, a popular cash crop.

For a quiet cup of coffee and stretch of legs, you can stop at Hotel Sonia, set back from the road in a mango orchard, or, if you are running late and into lunch time, try Giani Dhaba just before the town starts.

From here it is a short drive of 31km to Haldwani but the turn off to it is poorly marked 6km out of Rudrapur and if Pantnagar starts showing up on the milestones, you know you've missed it!

Haldwani, and its twin town Kathgodam, serve as the rail and road head for these hills. The journey through these towns, barely 6km apart, takes time as the narrow road is cluttered with two-wheeler and auto rickshaw traffic commuting between them. There are numerous hotels in the city but Woodpecker is popular for its spacious and quiet setting in a mango grove, while Udupi Café, just 2km beyond Kathgodam railway station, serves fresh idlis, dosas, delicious sambar and good South Indian coffee too!

It is from here that you start ascending and within the hour are in the 'Lake District of India' – Bhimtal is 21km away and Naukuchiyatal just 6km from it. This series of mountain lakes were also termed 'Westmorland of India' by the British. However, don't expect the same picture-postcard manicured prettiness; these lakes have a much wilder natural beauty, each with its own special appeal. The most popular of these enchanting lakes are Nainital, Bhimtal, Sat Tal, Panna (Garur) Tal and Naukuchiyatal.

Soon after Kathgodam, look out for signs and a

road to the right leading down to a bridge – this is the route to Bhimtal while the straight one takes you to Nainital (actually, a branch of this also connects up with our route at Bhowali, past Bhimtal).

The road to Bhimtal is quite curvaceous as you ascend to cooler climes at 4000ft/1220m quite rapidly. Approaching this small town you crest a hill to find the lake before you – a sight for 'traffic-strained' eyes! This is the largest of the Tals (lakes), and its calm waters reflect the surrounding hills and trees. The route runs along one bank of the lake but if you want to stop and soak in the sights and atmosphere, try Monolith

The sleepy railway station at Rampur

Resort that affords a great overview of the lake. To get to it you will have to make a sharp right after cresting the hill. The usual dhaba cluster and boat vendors crowd around the opposite bank as you come into Bhimtal. You have to circumvent the lake when you come in and take a sharp left turn for Naukuchiyatal. The last two kilometers of this short drive is on an unsurfaced road.

Naukuchiyatal is an enchanting smaller lake set amidst well-forested hills and takes its name from its shape – nine-cornered. You can choose one of the many hotels here to spend the night but we

Take a pedal or row boat onto the lake. If it's warm, you can take a dip to cool off but be prepared – the water can be a little chilly.

would certainly recommend Lake Resort which is a large property, beautifully spread along the lake – its buildings are sensitively set back, around lawns, rather than crowding the lake. The atmosphere at Naukuchiyatal is peaceful and when a breeze builds up, the soothing sound of the trees can lull you. If you are feeling energetic, you could enjoy a morning swim before the boats start to crowd the lake. There are great forest walks around here with interesting birdlife and some amazing butterflies so remember to carry a pair of binoculars ■

Naukuchiyatal, seen from the Lake Resort Hotel

DAY 2
▸▸ Visit Mukteshwar and Sat Tal

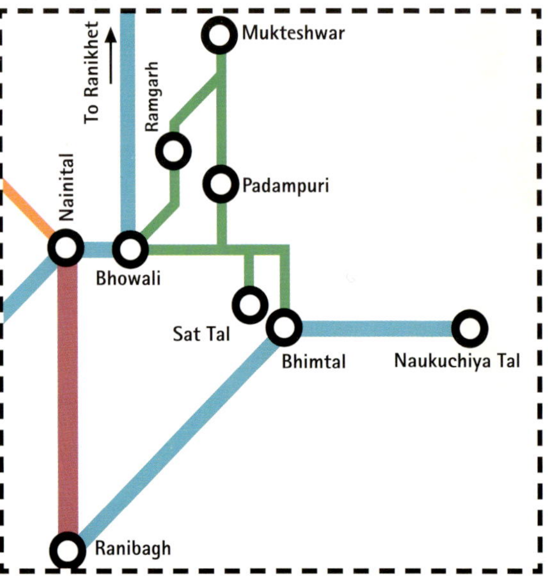

Naukuchiyatal-Mukteshwar	52 km	Naukuchiyatal-Sat Tal	17 km
Mukteshwar-Bhowali	43 km	Naukuchiyatal-Bhowali	15 km
Bhowali-Nainital	11 km		

There is a great forest walk from Mukteshwar to Sitla. Carry a picnic lunch and enjoy yourself in these pristine sylvan surroundings.

The second day involves a leisurely start after an optional morning stroll and a good breakfast. It is a 52km (2-2.5 hour) drive to Mukteshwar (7500ft/2287m), that boasts the most brilliant panoramic views of the Himalayas and is well known for its spectacular sunsets. The lawns of the PWD Rest House are an ideal viewing point and the slopes below it are covered in a thick rich forest that is wonderful to walk and explore. The British established the IVRI (Indian Veterinary Research Institute) at Mukteshwar in 1898 and there are some lovely colonial buildings along well maintained small roads. The library here has an interesting feature — the foot-rest for the

reading tables is a brass pipe that used to circulate hot water to keep your feet warm as you read! What consideration!!

You could either carry lunch and pick one of the many scenic spots for a picnic or try the local fare at Mountain Trail or the KMVN Tourist Rest House.

On your return, make a short 6km detour to Sat Tal, which actually comprises of seven interconnected tarns. The three main lakes are Ram, Laxman and Sita. Day-trippers, usually from Nainital, favour this lake and there are numerous dhabas as you approach it. Pedal boats also ply on this lake.

True to its name, the adjoining Panna (Garur) Tal is set like an emerald amidst forested hills. Quieter by far, the chirping of cicadas and birds with the occasional 'plop' of a fish in the lake adds to an immeasurable sense of peace. The still, deep waters are great to swim in.

You should now head back to your hotel at Naukuchiyatal for a relaxed evening. For those who do not mind being on the move, the option would be to pack up and leave in the morning for Sat Tal and Panna Tal and then drive up to the cooler heights of Mukteshwar for the night ■

Living up to its name — the emerald lake, Panna Tal

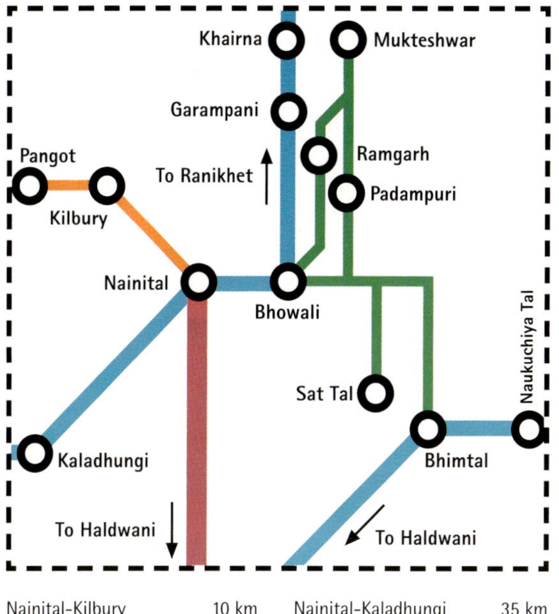

If you are in the mood for a quiet drive, take the road from Bhowali towards Ramgarh. Less than an hour away you cross Gaggar Pass into the 'fruit bowl of Kumaon'.

| Nainital-Kilbury | 10 km | Nainital-Kaladhungi | 35 km |
| Kilbury-Pangot | 3.5 km | | |

With Nainital only a short drive away, you can time your departure, after breakfast, to suit your convenience. Bhowali is 15km along an ascending road and a climb of another 11km brings you to Nainital (6400ft/1951m), the most popular hill station in Kumaon. The British identified the salubrious climate at Bhowali as ideal and set up one of the finest T.B. Sanitariums of the time over here. Today it is a major fruit market and travellers returning home typically stop to pick up the fine peaches, apricots and plums on sale here. En route to Nainital (3km short of it), on the left you will notice a crumbling arched stone entrance – this is an abandoned British cemetery. Although just off a busy road it seems locked in time and a walk through it, reading epitaphs on gravestones gives you a glimpse of an era gone by.

Nainital is overly built up and during season is grossly overrun with tourist and motor traffic and yet, incredibly, it retains its charm! There are several outlying sections that have withstood the ravages of time and 'progress' and it is here that you get a sense of how very beautiful this valley must have been. The weather is generally cool in the summer months with depressions over the lake sometimes bringing in mist and rain. Autumn and winter can be very cold.

The history of Nainital is fascinating, with all the machinations and elements of skullduggery that characterised the expansion of the British Raj.

Officially Nainital was 'discovered' in 1839 by a British sugar merchant Mr. P. Barron, even though the area had been under the control of the East India Company since 1815! Apparently the first commissioner of this region G.W. Traill, was aware of this beautiful, secluded (at that time!), lake but chose to keep the knowledge under wraps, possibly in deference to local religious sentiments. Suspicious that his guides were being deliberately vague and misleading about the existence of this lake, Barron concluded that this non-cooperation was at Traill's behest. He recorded his indignation: "– the late Commissioner of Kumaon who is said to have paid a visit to this lake many years ago, and, it is well known, possessed the most extraordinary influence among the natives of the hills and entertained peculiarly illiberal ideas regarding the influx of European visitors into the province –" (Pilgrim, 1844).

However, having discovered this Himalayan jewel that many likened to the Cumbrian lake district 'back home', Barron (under the pseudonym

You could refresh yourself with a hot or cold beverage at Country Inn or George's which lies just short of Bhowali.

'Pilgrim'), canvassed energetically for its development. He built a small cottage, which came to be known as 'Pilgrim's Cottage', and had plans to lay a European colony on the shores of the lake — a forerunner of the construction boom! But, all this only after Barron overcame what was for him a minor hiccup:

The local chieftain, Thokdar Nur Singh, laid claims on the lake and surrounding hills and objected to any intrusion on the sacred lake. Failing to win him over by fair means, Barron resorted to the ruthlessness of a true expansionist. He persuaded Nur Singh to row with him on the lake and somewhere in the middle threatened to

A gravestone in the overgrown British cemetery as you approach Nainital

SHIVA AND HIS COSMIC DANCE OF DEATH

Parvati, known as Sati in her previous incarnation, was the daughter of King Daksha and married Shiva against her father's wishes. Daksha organised a grand Yagna (ritual sacrifice), to which all and sundry were invited except his daughter and the son-in-law acquired by default. When Sati heard of this, she was deeply insulted at the humiliation inflicted on her husband and stormed into the ceremonial hall. Before her father's horrified eyes she jumped into the sacrificial fire and immolated herself (some accounts mention spontaneous combustion). This event is believed to have occurred at the spot where the Daksheswara Temple now stands at Kankhal (near Haridwar).

Hearing this enraged Shiva beyond measure and he stormed in with his trident ablaze and destroyed the sacrificial fire and injured many gods and demi-gods sitting there. The mayhem is described in the Puranas as "Indra is knocked down and trampled on, Yama has his staff broken, Saraswati and Matris have their noses wounded, Bhag has his eyes pulled out, Pushan has his teeth knocked down his throat, Chandra is pummeled, Agri's hands are broken, Bhragu's beard is crushed, Prajapatis are beaten and the gods are running around scared."

Shiva then gathered up the charred remains of his wife to carry her to his Himalayan abode at Mount Kailash. Torn with grief, he danced across the universe, unleashing primeval forces. The mountains tottered, the earth shook, the wind roared and the depth of the seas were disturbed. Indeed, the entire universe was threatened with destruction until the gods, led by Vishnu, cut Sati's body into pieces that were scattered all over India. The eyes are believed to have fallen by the side of the lake and hence the name Naini (eyes), Tal.

capsize the boat if he did not relinquish his claim
on the lake and lands. Unable to swim, the hapless
Nur Singh waived his claim on a written
document. In Barron's words, "The case was at this
time before either the Board of Revenue or
Government. On getting into the lake I asked him
if he would resign his Pretensions and admit the
right of the Hon'ble Company Bahadur to the lake
and intimated to him that he had his choice of
doing so or being left in possession of his property
on the spot. He looked very blank, said the lake
was very deep and agreed to waive his claim in
preference to the chance, or rather certainty, of
being drowned if the boat were upset; a feat we
assured him we could perpetrate in one instant
without danger to ourselves. Being always
provided with a book and pencil when in the hills,
I produced them and the poor man wrote out in it
a deed by which he resigned all claim to the lake.
All Paharees of Kumaon, however poor, can read
and write and as soon as we returned to the shore,
I exhibited this document to the assembled crowd".

After the takeover, many hill bungalows and
even mansions were built above the lake and the
township grew to be the summer capital of the
government of the United Provinces and recently
was a strong contender for the capital of
Uttarakhand.

Prior to these developments, Nainital was a place
of considerable religious significance for the local
people.

According to legend, when Shiva was carrying
the body of his consort Sati to Mount Kailash, her
eyes fell in this spot and hence Nainital was
regarded as a sacred place, revered and visited by
devout pilgrims.

A lesser-known anecdote regarding the origin of
the lake is mentioned in the *Skanda Purana* where

The Nainital Boat Club
has had a face lift and is
a great place to relax over
a drink with the water
lapping at your feet. Pick
up a book from Narain's
bookstore to add to the
mood!

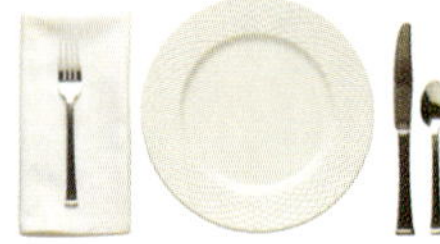

Dinner at the lofty heights of Manu Maharani, Fairhaven or Belvedere Hotel can be an enthralling experience with the stars above and twinkling lights of town below.

it is called the Tri-Rishi Sarovar. Three rishis (Atri, Pulastya and Pulaha), while on pilgrimage reached the base of the Naina peak but thirsty as they were, they could not find water to slake their thirst. Remembering the holy lake at Mansarovar they started digging a large pit, which miraculously filled with water from Mana. Later, after the legend of Sati's eyes it was re-christened to its present name.

Nainital is surrounded by seven hills known as the Sapta-Shring and has had its share of natural

disaster. In 1880 torrential rain led to a massive landslide at the northern end of the lake (Mallital). An overhanging cliff came down and buried the Victoria Hotel, Bell's Department Store and the Naina Devi Temple that were all located at this shore of the lake. Over 150 people lost their lives during this tragedy and subsequently this area was levelled and became known as the 'Flats'. It is now used as a cricket/football ground and as a place for public meetings.

While in Nainital, visit the beautiful church of

The deck of the Nainital Boat Club

St. John-in-the-Wilderness and the old British cemetery 3km out of town on the Bhowali road. The church was named by the Bishop of Calcutta during his visit in 1844 when, unlike today, this site was very much part of the wilderness. The church is one of the finest built in any hill station but is no longer in active use and opens only on Sunday evenings.

If you have not already stopped at it on the way in, the cemetery is certainly interesting. Two other churches, that of St. Francis and the Methodist Church, lie on the Mall and being in active use are much better preserved. Just below St. John is the impressive High Court building, formerly known as the Government House. Built in 1899, it

St. John-in-the-Wilderness, Nainital

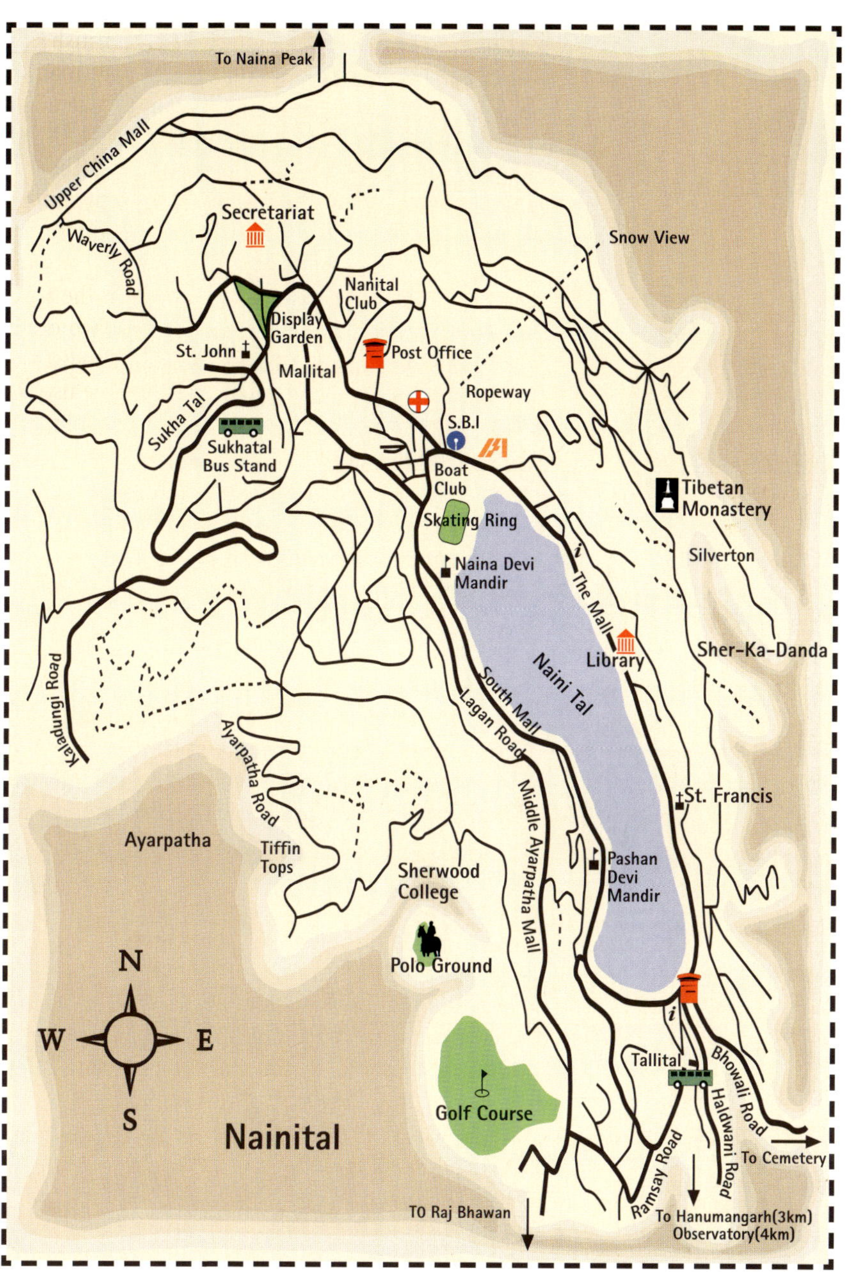

To Naina Peak
Upper China Mall
Waverly Road
Secretariat
Snow View
Nanital Club
Display Garden
St. John
Mallital
Post Office
Ropeway
Sukha Tal
S.B.I
Sukhatal Bus Stand
Boat Club
Tibetan Monastery
Skating Ring
Silverton
Naina Devi Mandir
The Mall
Library
Sher-Ka-Danda
Kaladhungi Road
Naini Tal
South Mall
Lagan Road
Ayarpatha Road
St. Francis
Ayarpatha
Tiffin Tops
Middle Ayarpatha Mall
Sherwood College
Pashan Devi Mandir
N
Polo Ground
W E
S
Tallital
Bhowali Road
Golf Course
Haldwani Road
To Cemetery
Nainital
Ramsay Road
To Raj Bhawan
To Hanumangarh(3km)
Observatory(4km)

Nainital's hillsides are studded with prestigious residential schools — including the 'Great B', Amitabh Bachchan's alma mater, Sherwood College.

was designed by F.W. Stephens who was also responsible for the famous Victoria Terminus and Churchgate railway stations in Mumbai. The building belongs to what is described as the 'early domestic Gothic style', but unfortunately it can now only be viewed from the fence surrounding its perimeter.

You can also take the cable car (officially, the 'Aerial Express'!), to a spot unimaginatively named 'Snow View'. On a clear day you have an excellent panoramic view of the Himalayas from here, with the snow capped Nanda Devi and its twin peak Nanda East flanked by Trishul on the left and the five Panchachuli peaks on the right.

If you are feeling energetic it is a pleasant 2km walk down to the Mall, past the Gadhan Kunkyop Ling Gompa of the Gelugpa sect that reveres the Dalai Lama as its spiritual head. This tiny monastery is surrounded by colourful prayer flags and serves the small Tibetan community settled here. The other, more strenuous option from Snow View is to walk up to China Peak (colloquially referred to as 'Cheena Peak'!), which at 8561ft/2610m is the highest point in this region.

Another good walk leads West of the lake (4km) to Dorothy's Seat, named after a memorial seat built by a Mr. Keller for his wife, killed in an air crash. It is a lovely walk through oak, pine and deodar forests from here to Lands End.

The Nainital Boat Club has undergone major renovation and has a pleasant lounge overlooking the lake. Temporary membership is available for visitors at a charge. It is a charming place to relax over a cup of coffee, or chilled beer, gaze at the emerald waters of the lake and wonder at Nainital as it must have been!

From the opposite end of the lake (Tallital), you can drive up to the Hanuman Temple (3km away) and then a kilometer further to the State Observatory. Sunset views are particularly good from the temple and you can indulge in some genuine stargazing through the telescope at the Observatory – but do check their timings in advance. The Raj Bhavan is a majestic building set in beautiful lawns and bordered by stately old deodars and other varieties of trees. It is often open for public viewing and boasts a magnificent 18-hole golf course with limited access to the public – with a bit of luck you could swing in a round or two!

A LITTLE OUT OF TOWN

This is after all Corbett's haunt and while in Nainital, do not miss the opportunity to drive through the dense verdant jungle just a few kilometers out of town. The nearest section, (10km

The Himalayas, viewed from above Nainital

away), is the drive to the Kilbury Forest Rest House that enjoys spectacular views. Carry a picnic hamper to Kilbury or proceed a little further (3.5km) to Pangot village. Just off and above the road, a short walk leads you to a resort that is a great place to stay out of town if that is what you enjoy. Run by an enterprising young couple it has mainly tented accommodation (though there are some rooms in the main house), and enjoys a lofty location midst cultivated fields bordered by forests and is immensely peaceful. You could stop for a cup of coffee and some quiet — or even choose to stay far from the madding crowd!

It may be worth your while to check out Mountain Quail Camp at Pangot — its fantastic location and the peace and quiet may tempt you to stay here the next time you are in the area!

The road continues through dense forest for another 35km or so and this is a great way to spend a day away from the touristy hustle-bustle of Nainital! The mountain views are also excellent, particularly between the 8 and 10km 'milestones', out of town. If you are up early, the view from here is even better than that from Snow View and you can pick your own spot to sit and relax without being jostled by the ever-increasing number of tourists arriving every ten minutes on the cable car. Another pleasant excursion is the drive to Kaladhungi (35km) where the Jim Corbett Museum is located ■

Not a fairytale castle but the Nainital High Court!

DAY 4 & 5
▸▸ Around Nainital and drive to Ranikhet

Nainital-Bhowali	11 km	Khairna-Ranikhet	30 km
Bhowali-Khairna	18 km	Khairna-Almora	33 km

Nainital is better stocked for exotic foods than any of your onward destinations. Pick up what you need as there are several occasions when picnic lunches are called for.

You can spend part of the day in or around Nainital covering the sites of interest that you weren't able to on the previous day. It is a short 59km (approximately 2 hour) drive via Bhowali to the picturesque and completely unspoilt hill retreat of Ranikhet. Bhowali (5500ft/1677m), is only 11km from Nainital and its busy, crowded market is the place to pick up luscious local fruit. However from here the drive goes down hill — literally — as you descend almost 2000ft/610m to the rather warm village of Garampani! En route you pass the nursery and retail outlet 'Plantiss', which has a variety of beautiful flowers and plants that you can admire or buy.

A short distance ahead is the Kainchi Mandir

Rich deodar forest

dedicated to the sage Baba Neem Karauli. This is a popular modern temple and ashram. Devotees throng here in huge numbers for the annual 'puja', often paralysing the flow of traffic for hours on end.

You arrive at the low point of the drive 8km further at Khairna (3100ft/940m). It lies at the confluence of the Kosi and the Uttarbahini (so named because it flows to the north). Beyond the market there is a bridge across the river and you turn left for Ranikhet. Driving straight ahead would take you to the very crowded and built-up township of Almora — not one of our

Beautiful potted begonias adorn Meghdoot Hotel, Ranikhet

recommended destinations! From Khairna Bridge it is a steadily ascending 30km or so drive to your destination at 6000ft/1829m. Unfortunately the hillsides are comparatively barren but the good road surface makes the drive bearable. After paying a toll tax at Pilkholi you cross the small hamlet of Panyali and a short distance ahead, (7km before Ranikhet), the road forks — take the ascending road up towards the Ranikhet post office. Your route beyond this point depends on where you intend to stay; the Ranikhet Club and main bazaar lie ahead while hotels such as West View, Rosemount and the Tourist Reception Center (KMVN) lie in the opposite direction.

Ranikhet (literally translated, means 'Queen's Field'), owes its name to an unknown Katyuri queen of the twelfth century who was travelling in this area. She was seduced by the green glades and awesome snow vistas and persuaded her husband to build her a home in this beautiful place. Though she visited the place regularly the 'khets' remained with the local populace till the British decided to establish a military cantonment here in 1869. The Katyuri queen was not the only one to be captivated by this area — Lord Mayo, one of the viceroys of India, planned to shift the summer capital here from Shimla but fortunately this did not come to pass. For the most part Ranikhet has retained its pristine charm and this is due to the fact that it is still predominantly a military cantonment. The regulatory authority, the Cantonment Board, has a reasonably strict set of rules regarding renovation and construction of buildings leased out by them as well as for land and forest under their control. They have been quite successful in preserving the environment in this area. Barring a 2km or so stretch of marketplace that is 'chak-a-chak' with little shops,

While in Ranikhet indulge your sweet tooth and try 'Bal Mithai', a local delicacy. Rich brown and fudge-like, it is delicious. You can pick it up at Hari Mishtan Bhandar opposite the petrol pump.

St. Martin's Church, Ranikhet

hotels, restaurants, teeming crowds and chaotic traffic, the rest of the town is quiet and peaceful. The famous Kumaon Regimental Center is headquartered at Ranikhet.

Besides its unspoilt character, Ranikhet also affords spectacular views of the snowcapped higher reaches of the Himalayas. The Mall and the area leading up to Chaubatia is well forested with pine and oak. The houses around here are from a long bygone age — charming, old-style colonial bungalows with deep verandahs and large gardens, often wearing a somewhat run-down air that adds just the right flavour to the untouched beauty of the place. Perhaps no other hill station offers such a grand panoramic view, starting in

the East with the Api-Nampi peaks of Nepal and the five Panchachuli summits all the way across a range of magnificent peaks to Kamet, bordering Tibet, in the West. Trishul (23,354ft/7120m) dominates the skyline, flanked on the left by Nanda Ghunti and the main Nanda Devi peak to the right, with her 'face' quite easily discernible from here. These majestic peaks take on a warm golden hue at dawn only to change to a brilliant white during the day and finally don a mysterious lilac-rose cloak at sunset — if you are lucky, you can even catch them shimmering silver in an inky sky during full moon nights!

Ranikhet offers you a quintessential hill holiday, as it used to be — the right atmosphere to relax

Sunset view of Mt. Trishul from the golf course

KUMAON REGIMENTAL CENTER

The Kumaon Regiment is one of India's finest and ironically has its roots miles away in Hyderabad, the capital of Andhra Pradesh. It was initially known as the Hyderabad Regiment and it was in 1780 that a Kumaoni Battalion was raised to serve in the erstwhile Hyderabad state. The first two battalions were known as Russell's Brigade and were used to quell the terror unleashed by the pindaris (bandits), who roamed central India between 1812-1818.

In 1853, the armed forces under the Nizam of Hyderabad were merged with those of the East India Company and these regiments were used in suppressing the 1857 freedom uprising. As part of the campaign, they were also responsible for defeating the forces of the illustrious Rani of Jhansi. The regiment was then absorbed as part of the regular British Army. It was only after the First World War that, for the first time, the Fourth Kumaon Regiment recruited Indian officers who had been trained at Sandhurst in England. Two of these young officers later went on to become the chiefs of the Indian Army — Generals S.M. Srinagesh and K.S. Thimaya. With the advent of the Second World War, these battalions were involved in fighting the

Japanese forces in Burma and on our eastern borders. In October 1945, the name of the regiment was finally changed from the Hyderabad Regiment to Kumaon Regiment and Col. Srinagesh became its first Indian commanding officer. The regiment soon found itself in the thick of action when an army of Lashkar tribesmen, backed by Pakistan, invaded Kashmir in 1948. At the decisive Battle of Badgam, it was a company of the Fourth Kumaon Regiment that saved the airfield from falling into enemy

The main Parade Ground, named after the KRC hero, Maj. Som Nath Sharma

hands. Led by Maj. Som Nath Sharma, the heavily outnumbered Kumaonis stuck it out till reinforcements arrived though the brave Maj. Sharma was killed in action. He was the first soldier to receive the Param Vir Chakra, India's highest decorative award for gallantry. The main parade ground at Ranikhet is named after this valiant officer. The year 1948 marks the shift of its regimental headquarters to Ranikhet, where it continues to be located to this day.

The Kumaon Regimental Center saw action during the 1962 war with China as also in the 1965 one with Pakistan. The regiment played an important role in the 1971 liberation of Bangladesh, fighting on both the eastern and western fronts. Its members proved their mettle yet again in the 1999 Kargil conflict — a war arena in which they played a key role.

A little known fact about the regiment is its important contribution to the local economy. In hundreds of surrounding villages at least one member of the family has served or is serving in the Kumaon Regiment. Recruited at the tender age of eighteen and retired at thirty-five, their salaries and pensions provide a major boost to the economy.

While in Ranikhet, you are certain to come across young recruits undergoing their 36-week long basic training – you cannot help but admire the spirit of these boys who look like they just made it to the 'teens'! In 1999, it was a heart rending sight seeing these youngsters riding in the back of trucks on their way to participate in the Kargil war, knowing well that many of them would end up as canon fodder.

In case you need to have your vehicle looked at, Sharif's garage (near Hari Mishtan) has stood the test of time and you are assured an honest and reliable assessment of your problem.

and chill out, take long walks in the forest, read, gaze at the mountains and indulge in meaningful conversation and maybe a game of Scrabble!

For those looking for things to do, a short visit to the Jhuladevi Temple would be interesting. The perimeter wall, as well as the courtyard, is surrounded by bells of every conceivable size! According to local tradition, a bell is tied when a wish made comes true and judging from the number of bells, this certainly seems like the right place to make a wish!

From here, it is a short but extremely scenic drive up to the fruit orchards at Chaubatia, also a cantonment station. In fact, once perusing a fascinating old British catalogue from the 'Army & Navy Store' (British families in far flung colonies could order in items from this – ranging from corsets to candelabras!), it was interesting to find a station code for even the small cantonment of Chaubatia! You can drive up to the viewpoint which has a café – don't let its garish touristy look put you off if you are in the mood for coffee.

There is a pleasant walk in the adjacent forest that leads you to the artificial Bhalu Dam, this was the main water source for Ranikhet. This man-made lake is only 3km away but barely a kilometer further, the path descends quite sharply to it and unless you are comfortable making the long haul back up, it is best to branch off at this point. A short (100m) walk along the ridge leads you to an ideal spot for a picnic lunch. At the entrance to the orchard, near the parking lot, is a shop that sells fresh produce as well as flowers and plant saplings. The orchards look fantastic when in blossom or richly laden with fruit. It is also possible to walk back to the Mall through beautiful thick forest on a narrow trail.

Sundowners!

Ranikhet has two lovely perambulatory walks in the Mall area; the more frequented and inhabited Mall Road section from Meghdoot Hotel to West View Hotel and the more secluded but prettier one starting from West View Hotel going past Jhuladevi Temple. The first walk takes you past many of the gracious bungalows originally built by the British and the complete round is approximately 3km long. The second route is somewhat shorter and is a 2km round. On the other side of the town, there is an Army Golf Course that lies 4km from the market, on the road to Almora. This was originally laid out as a cross-country track by British officers but was later converted into a 9-hole golf course. Golfers can play a couple of rounds on this course by paying a nominal fee. A set of clubs can be hired as also

The Golf Course at Kalika, Ranikhet

the services of caddies and 'ageywalahs', whose importance cannot be underestimated as slightly wayward shots will disappear into the forest surrounding this amazing course! During the monsoons you can get some stunning sunset views from here.

Just ahead of the golf course is the Kalika Temple dedicated to the goddess Kalika (a representation of Kali), who is the patron saint of the Kumaon Regiment. Majkhali, a village that lies 6km ahead, is possibly one of the best spots in this area for unhindered panoramic views of the snow peaks that appear to be even closer from here!

Ranikhet also has some interesting old churches that date back to the early nineteenth century but only two or three are in active use. One abandoned church, located just above the Narsing

'Ring my bell' — Jhuladevi Temple

With an extensive menu Windsor Lodge offers the best cuisine in Kumaon! Try Rosemount Hotel for chicken/paneer sizzlers. Sati's dhaba, near the bus stand is good for a quick snack.

Stadium, has been converted to an AWWA retail outlet and production center for good quality shawls and tweed fabrics. These are woven by army wives and widows under the aegis of the KRC welfare scheme. Shoppers will certainly welcome a stop here as the prices and quality are good and the tweed especially interesting. Another impressive structure is the Methodist Church that lies at the other end of town, just ahead of the Som Nath Parade Ground.

Trishul, as viewed from Dunagiri

Being the headquarter of the Kumaon Regimental Center, Ranikhet boasts a fine museum that traces the history of the regiment from its inception to the present. Located above the S.D.M's office (Sub-Divisional Magistrate), it is well worth a visit if one has any interest in military history.

Another interesting visit could be to the ashram and temple of Haidakhan Wale Baba at Chilianaula, just 4km from the market ■

BABA HAIDAKHAN WALE

According to popular belief, Baba Haidakhan Wale was a 'maha avtar' — a human manifestation of the Divine, not born of woman — who has been continually manifesting as a divine body on this earth since the beginning of creation. He is said to have unhesitatingly acknowledged that he was Shiva Maha avtar Babaji described by Paramhansa Yogananda in his book, *Autobiography of a Yogi'*.

Yogananda believed "Great prophets like Christ and Krishna come to earth for a specific and spectacular purpose; they depart as soon as it is accomplished. Other avtars like Babaji undertake work that is concerned with the slow evolutionary progress of man during the centuries rather than with any one outstanding event of history. Such masters always veil themselves from the crass public gaze and have the power to become invisible at will. For these reasons and because they generally instruct the disciples to maintain silence about them, a number of towering spiritual figures remain unknown".

His manifestation of 1970 is supposed to be one of a series of continuous appearances for over eighteen centuries. Prior to this, his last recorded appearance was in the eighteenth century when he spent considerable time in the Kumaon region. Tibetan lamas who met him at that time recognised him as one who had lived in Tibet centuries ago. He left this form in 1922, dematerialising himself in a ball of light while seated on the confluence of the Kali and Gori Ganga rivers — an event apparently witnessed by many of his devotees.

The learned Mahendra Maharaj and Nantin Baba foretold the latest manifestation. In 1970, this strapping 18-year old youth was spotted near a cave at the base of Adi Kailash Mountain in Haidakhan, Kumaon's northern border with Nepal. In September 1970, he ascended Mount Kailash and sat on the summit for forty-five days without food or sleep, thus establishing his yogic powers. He spent most of the fourteen years in this incarnation at Haidakhan, where he added nine temples to the original that was built in the year 1800. In Ranikhet, he set up an ashram and built a temple in the outlying village of Chilianaula.

The principal belief of the followers of Haidakhan Wale Baba is the revival of the ageless religion, Sanatan Dharma, to reform the psychology of man by laying stress on three basic precepts — truth, simplicity and love. The belief is that in this era of 'Kalyug', mankind is in grave moral danger from rising materialism and the simultaneous decline of spiritual faith. Only those who worship God with sincerity and repeat his name by chanting 'Om Namah Shivay' (I bow to God), will survive.

In February 1984, he departed from his mortal body and his last message "I am always with you" is inscribed on a stone near the steps of the Haidakhan Temple. He preached selfless service to humanity as the highest form of 'karamyog' and in deference to his wish, a charitable hospital is being run at Chilianaula and Haidakhan for the improvement of the health of Kumaoni people.

An altar to Babaji inside the temple

DAYS 6 & 7
▸▸ Excursions from Ranikhet
TO DWARAHAT, DUNAGIRI AND MAYBE PANDUKHOLI

At Ranikhet check out the hand knitted sweaters, natural honey and exotic jams made by a hill women's co-operative, Mahila Umang. Their outlet is in Naini village, around 4km from Kalika, but their products are available at the AWWA shop at the Tweed Center.

Ranikhet-Dwarahat	33 km	Majkhali-Kathpuria	8 km
Dwarahat-Dunagiri	14 km	Kathpuria-Sitlakhet	9 km
Ranikhet-Kalika	6 km	Kathpuria-Kosi	13 km
Kalika-Majkhali	6 km	Kosi-Almora	12 km
Ranikhet-Chaubatia	9 km		

Dwarahat, 33km from Ranikhet, lies in a valley and is at a somewhat lower elevation. This was originally a capital of the Katyuri dynasty and you should stop to see remnants of the temples built here by them in the eleventh century. There were around sixty temples divided into eight groups but these ceased to be active places of worship after the Rohilla army desecrated them in the eighteenth century. Three of these temples, including the Mrityunjaya and Badrinath temples, lie in fields adjacent to the road. Though the

One of the abandoned
temples at Dwarahat

temples follow a standard, rather simple structural line, some of the carvings and workmanship on the idols is still exquisite inspite of neglect and erosion having obscured the more delicate nuances. This temple complex is now under the supervision of the ASI (Archaeological Survey of India).

From here it is a 14km drive to the base of Dunagiri Temple that enjoys a magnificent view of the Himalayan range. This temple is dedicated to Vaishno Devi. The one kilometer climb from the main road is on a gentle gradient over a series of approximately 364 broad steps. According to

Part of the Katarmal Temple complex

legend, when Hanuman was flying back to Lanka with the Sanjivani Buti required to treat Laxman, he dropped a bit of the herb here and since that day the place was known as Dunagiri. Another belief holds that when the buti fell here, an iron grass-cutting sickle turned to gold, establishing the special sanctity of the place. The bronze plate in the temple is believed to date back to 1181.

The road ends 6km further but for those interested in a bit of uphill walking, it is a 5km (2 hours) hike to the top of Pandukholi from where there are great views on a clear day. The name is derived from the legend that during the period of their 'agyat vas', the Pandavas lived here in a cave. With an early start, and great deal of enthusiasm, you can climb to Pandukholi, have a picnic lunch and either visit Dunagiri (if you have your climbing legs still intact!), or just stop to see the ancient roadside temple ruins of Dwarahat.

▶▶ To Katarmal Sun Temple, Sitlakhet Forest and the Temple of Syahidevi

Sitlakhet Forest is a 26km drive from Ranikhet, past Majkhali and on the road towards Almora. From the village of Kathpuria you turn right on a narrow winding climb of around 9km. Sitlakhet has a beautiful forest and very few visitors (other than when iDiscovery runs camps for school children), and makes an ideal place for a picnic lunch and to spend the day. From here, the Syahi Devi Temple is a gentle 3km walk each way. A natural spring at this spot was the main source of water for Almora seventy years ago and this place was revered as the 'saviour of Almora'.

Another ideal spot for a day trip is the ancient sun temple at Katarmal. It is approximately 36km from Ranikhet on the road to Almora and is a pleasant drive through dense and medium forests,

We would advise you not to take your vehicle up the very rough road leading to Katarmal. When we did so a couple who were trudging up made it only five minutes after us!

Try your luck at leopard spotting. After dusk, take a drive along the 'back road' of the Mall, past Rosemount Hotel and on to Jhula Devi Temple — this is leopard country.

with occasional snow views, till you reach the unlikely milestone reading 'Katarmal-0' with no signs of temple or habitation! Almost a kilometer further (and approximately 2km before Kosi) is a rough path on the right leading up to Katarmal. After a steep climb of almost one kilometer, the 'road' gets rougher and rockier as you ascend till it gives up pretenses altogether — luckily at a spot where you can turn the car around! There are a few places before this point where you can stop (and be able to turn) if the road is getting unmanageable. Alternatively, if you don't feel like testing your driving skills and decide to walk all the way, remember to carry drinking water.

After you have parked at the last point, it is a gentle walk of almost a kilometer to the temple complex. The Katarmal village has a lofty perch with series of hills and valleys spread before it — there is a quiet serenity about the place as life goes indoors at dusk.

The ancient temples are above the village on a spur and look like they have been hewn from the hill's rock face. Built 900 years ago, during the reign of the Katyuri dynasty, this edifice has an imposing and timeless air about it. The complex had forty-four temples but the one dedicated to God Surya (Bara Aditya), was the most famous, being the only Sun temple in the region. The main idol of the Sun God is now at the National Museum in Delhi but even the image you see within the temple is magnificent — it has Surya Devta on his chariot, led by his seven horses and the 'navgraha' (nine planets) depicted around him. There is a wooden 'shaktipeeth' behind it. Your efforts at getting here are justified by just a glimpse of this unusual statue!

Currently the complex is being renovated by the ASI and is a beehive of activity during the day.

Work on the 'shikhar' of the main Sun temple is just starting and one sincerely hopes the restoration is done sensitively, retaining its 'well-aged' appearance rather than a freshly cemented finish!

The best way to plan your day would be a morning visit to Katarmal, followed by a relaxed lunch in the verdant forest of Sitlakhet and a walk up to Syahi Devi Temple, if you wish, before returning to Ranikhet.

This is your last night in Ranikhet as the next day takes you to the elaborate temples at Jageshwar. You can make a relaxed start as the drive is only two hours or so ■

All you can hear is the sound of birds....

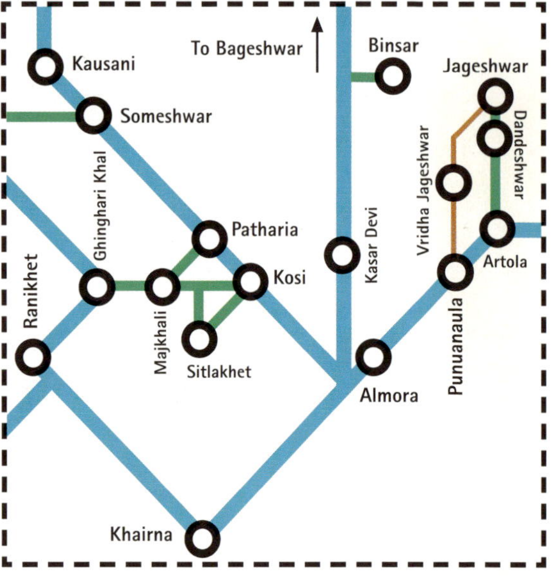

The approach to Almora is a hot one. You descend sharply to cross the Kosi River and the drive from there is on a pretty barren hill face.

Ranikhet-Almora via		Ranikhet-Almora via	
Majkhali	45 km	Khairna	63 km
Almora-Jageshwar	34 km	Almora-Binsar	32 km

This day involves a 45km drive to Almora, the former capital of the Chand dynasty, and then on to a spectacular complex of fifty-four temples at Jageshwar. It is a three and a half hour drive out and you have the option of spending the night at Binsar/Almora or returning to Ranikhet.

Almora is located on Kashaya Hill that is mentioned in the *Skanda Purana* as being the abode of Lord Vishnu. In the past Almora enjoyed considerable power and importance as the capital of the Chand kings but now it has little to recommend itself besides administrative control, being the district headquarters. It has grown into an overbuilt and crowded township with few

Inside the Jageshwar
complex

havens left of the quiet, forested beauty it was known for. Almora is one of the few hill stations the British did not have to build but while their stamp is visible on the main post office building, the clock tower is a confusion of architectural styles. There is a temple dedicated to Nanda Devi in a small complex next to the bus stand.

When G.H. Traill was the commissioner, the temple was shifted to another site and it is believed that due to this sacrilegious act he was punished and lost his eyesight while traversing the Pindari Glacier. To make amends, the temple was promptly moved back and Traill miraculously regained his vision! (In all likelihood an acute case of snow blindness, but the legend lives on...).

Copperware from Almora was famous in the past and artisans of this traditional craft can still be

Traditional wood carving, 'likhai', on a window

found in the Tamta Mohalla. In the nearby Khazanchi Mohalla, there are a number of attractive buildings, in the traditional Pahari architectural style, with beautifully carved wooden windows and doors. The highest point of the bazaar is where the Collectorate is situated; this is actually the old Almora Fort and there is a good view of the town and surrounding hills from here. On one of the buildings is an inscription "Fort Nanda Devi erected by the Chand Rajas and strengthened by the Gorkha government, captured by the British under Col. Nichols on April 26th, 1815". The convention for the surrender of Kumaon was formed the next day.

Almora became a popular hang out for the hippies of the 1960s and '70s; they frequented an area known as 'Crank's Ridge' that lies 6km out of town near the ancient Kasar Devi Temple.

Before the influx of these foreigners, Swami Vivekanand spent some time here. Later during the Quit India Movement, the British incarcerated our first prime minister, Pandit Jawaharlal Nehru in Almora. The famous writer, D.H. Lawrence also spent two summers in this town. Other luminaries who visited it were Timothy Leary (father of the 'hippy' movement who also pioneered the use of LSD, the psychedelic drug), singers Bob Dylan and Cat Stevens. Obviously it was not just the salubrious climate and quiet atmosphere but the cannabis (charas) plant, growing in wild abundance, which was the real lure!

You can also stop at the Govind Ballabh Pant Museum, as this is the only one in the Kumaon region. It contains an exquisite collection of ancient artifacts dating back to the eleventh century as also samples of traditional Kumaoni arts and crafts. Six kilometers from Almora, on a hilltop, is the Chitai Temple, dedicated to Lord

Almora is the last big town on your 'Himalayan Odyssey'. From now on you will be staying in smaller but far more beautiful places. Keep your camera ready.

Golu, with a shrine decorated with a canopy of bells.

A great place for sunrise and sunset views is Brighton End Corner on the Mall. (Though why the British, nostalgic or otherwise, would choose to name this spot after their favourite beach resort will remain a mystery!).

Both the Garhwal and the Kumaoni kings revered Nanda Devi and the temple dedicated to her draws people from all over, especially during the annual festival and fair held here every August/September.

This goddess is supposed to be the Kumaoni incarnation of Parvati, the wife of Shiva. According to local legend Nanda and Sunanda, the daughters of a local chieftain, were gored to death by a mad buffalo. Nanda made her abode in the icy reaches of the highest peak in this region subsequently named Nanda Devi after her. She is believed to live there with her husband, Shiva, through the year and descends annually to visit her maternal home. The festival marks her return to her husband's abode at the end of this visit and she is sent off with gifts, amidst fanfare and tears of farewell.

It is believed that she requested a buffalo be sacrificed to her since it was this species that harmed her in her earlier avtar and that is why a buffalo sacrifice was part of the festivities. Later, the sacrifice ('bali') was changed to that of the more affordable goat and is now quite often substituted with an offering of coconuts. The festival is celebrated with great pomp in Almora and extends into three consecutive days and nights. Songs and 'jagars' (religious chanting) are sung around a sacred fire to the frenzied beat of the 'hurka' (drums) and it is a very impressive performance. The spirit of Nanda Devi is believed

If you want to spend time in Almora, we recommend doing so when you can witness the Nanda Devi Festival, held in August / September every year.

THE LEGEND OF GOLU DEVTA

In ancient times, the Katyuri King Jhalrai was out on a hunt and after a hard day out, sent his servants to fetch some water. They found a water fall and while filling their vessels splashed and disturbed a young woman, Kali, who was meditating nearby. On seeing this beautiful serene woman, the king fell in love at first sight and insisted on marrying her. She became his favourite Rani (queen), much to the chagrin of the other queens. When Kali was pregnant, the king was delighted but it so happened he was away when the baby was born and the other queens decided to vent their jealousy on the unsuspecting Kali. They sedated her and kidnapped the baby, substituting it with a pumpkin they tucked into the crib. The baby was put in a basket and set afloat on the river. He was found by a childless fisherman who took the baby to be a boon granted from God and brought him up as his own. The child was named Golu or Goril, after the river Gori Ganga where he was found.

Some years later Golu wandered upstream with his toy horse and came to a spot where the queens were bathing. With childish innocence, he asked the queens to move aside so his toy horse could drink water. The Ranis scoffed him and asked how a wooden horse could drink water and were shocked to hear Golu respond that if a queen could give birth to a pumpkin, surely a wooden horse could drink water! Word of this incident got back to the king and he immediately understood that this boy was his true heir apparent and guessed what had actually taken place at his birth. Kali was reinstated in favour and Golu brought to the palace. He later became a great general in the king's army and subsequently succeeded his father to the throne and ruled with great impartiality and fairness. He is now revered as the Kumaoni god of justice and the pile of petitions in a corner of the temple, waiting for him to mete justice, are testimony to the people's belief in him. When a wish is granted, bells large and small are hung and there is a virtual canopy of them. Some years ago, someone actually put up a 500kg bell!! As you drive along, you will see the slogan 'Jai Golu Devta' on many of the local vehicles and Chitai Temple is constantly thronged by supplicants and grateful devotees.

to enter the body of a male oracle who is borne on the shoulders of a group of men. He begins by solving village problems on behalf of the Devi, but with the intensifying drum beats, goes into a trance; his body jerks in spasms, arms flail and eyes almost pop out of their sockets. In this state, he has to be forcibly restrained from leaping off his perch into the pyre! Clenched in his teeth is a small dagger symbolising the belief that the voice of Devi will not be muffled or let any one get in the way. As the pitch reaches a crescendo, the drummers also seem possessed and mothers hold up their children to be blessed by the 'goddess' — quite an awesome spectacle!

There are two optional routes to Almora from Ranikhet and involve a drive of either 45km of 63km.

One route takes you back on the road you entered Ranikhet by — down to the Kosi River at Khairna Bridge and then left towards Almora (63km). This drive takes less time since it is not as curvaceous.

The other one is more scenic as for the most part you drive through pine and oak forest with good snow views. You drive out of town, past the rolling greens of the golf course, past Majkhali and down to the Kosi River just before Almora.

Jageshwar (6429ft/1960m), is 34km from Almora and takes around an hour to reach. Before you reach Jageshwar, 2km beyond Punuanaulah and 3km before Artola, there is an 8km long, slightly rough dirt track on the left hand side. This takes you through dense forest to the Vridha (old) Jageshwar Temple perched on a hilltop almost 2000ft/610m above the main complex. This original stone temple, dedicated to Lord Shiva, has an aura of peace, tranquility and strong spiritual vibrations.

Don't be disheartened by the relatively boring and uninspiring drive for the initial 30km or so — the temples at Jageshwar more than compensate!

A short 1.5km track brings you to Hiriya Shikhar (7708ft/2350ms), which has brilliant views of the Himalayan range with the peaks of eastern Garhwal stretching right up to those in western Nepal, visible on a clear day. Once you are back on the main road, around a kilometer ahead look for a sign on the right hand side which points to some stone-age caves with wall paintings. These caves are just off the road and have primitive paintings in natural colours of red, black and white, depicting human figures, trees and animals – mute testimony to possibly the earliest inhabitants of the area.

From Artola you turn off the main road and after a short 2km drive the landscape changes dramatically. The valley you enter has huge deodar trees with dappled sunlight filtering

Nanda Devi at sunset, viewed from Auli

through, catching the movement of the stream as it rushes by – a beautiful verdant forest. As you savour the beauty of it all, you come upon the Dandeshwar group of temples in this idyllic setting. This is possibly one of the most peaceful spots to truly appreciate the magnificence of our ancient temple heritage and you begin to understand why learned men and spiritual gurus chose such places of beauty to build their dedication to the gods. The largest temple of this group dates back to the tenth century. It is

The Jageshwar Temple complex

elaborately sculpted and holds a naturally formed lingam. You can stop to see the complex on the way in, or when headed back and pick a nice spot around it for a peaceful picnic lunch.

Another kilometer or so through dense forest, brings you to the main Jageshwar Temple complex. In recent years, this has become more crowded and touristy with rows of shops and persistent pandits and is sadly going the way of other religious centers like Haridwar, where peace and tranquility is a thing of the past. However, to

A half hour drive on a gravel track leads you to the small Vridh Jageshwar Temple. Sans tourists, a visit to this peaceful place is a good way to end your pilgrimage here.

JYOTIR LINGAMS

There are two legends regarding the origin of the Jyotir Lingams. There was an argument between Brahma and Vishnu over who was the greatest and when they failed to arrive at a conclusion, the earth split apart to reveal a huge incandescent pillar of light. They tried to find the ends of this light – Vishnu became a boar and burrowed underground while Brahma took to the skies in the form of an eagle. After a thousand cosmic years of fruitless searching, Shiva finally emerged from the lingam of light. Both Vishnu and Brahma readily conceded that Shiva was the greatest, thus bringing the dispute to a conclusion. Shiva is thus the infinite light (Jyoti) and the Jyotir Lingam represents the atma (soul) — the infinite and eternal light; the light of truth, knowledge and illumination. The lingam is the energy of creation with the rounded stone symbolising the dome of the sky. The phallic symbol set within the 'yoni' represents the male-female energies. The Jyotir Lingam derives energy and power (shakti) from within itself unlike the other lingams, which have mantra shakti invested in them by the priests.

The other legend relates to the time that Shiva was in penance for the destruction caused during his raging cosmic dance while carrying Sati's body. He was in deep meditation at Vridh Jageshwar when the wives of seven sages came across him while collecting fodder. They were awestruck by the power and beauty of this unknown rishi with dreadlocks. Rooted to the spot (and by some accounts rendered unconscious), they failed to return home in the evening. Their husbands came in search and not recognising Shiva, cursed him for capturing their wives' attention. Shiva suffered the curse and a great darkness descended over the world. It was left to Vishnu to set matters right and he gathered up the darkness and dispersed it by forming the twelve Jyotir Lingams which are held in great reverence.

be fair, the complex is awesome and the temple architecture will certainly make you forget other inconveniences. This is the site of one of the twelve Jyotir Lingams – the Swayambhu Lingam – and holds special sanctity.

This complex, known as the Jageshwar Samuh, encompasses 124 temples, the oldest of which dates back to the eighth century. According to popular mythology of the region, it was here the Rishi Markand chanted the Mahamrityunjaya incantations. Ravana performed penance here to appease Lord Shiva; the Pandavas visited this holy site as did the Adi Shankaracharya many years later.

Built in the Nagara style, the temples have tall curvilinear spires (shikhars) surmounted by a Amolaka (capstone), topped by the Kalash (crown). The oldest temple is the Mahamrityunjaya Temple with elaborate carvings on its sides. A round medallion on the front represents Dattatreya, the three faces of one god. Below this is a carving of Lord Shiva flanked by Parvati and his son Kartikeya. Since he is depicted in the 'padmasana' (yogic lotus position), some infer to the pervasive influence of Buddhism, even though this religion was on the wane.

The other large temple, towering over numerous others, lies on the left and this is the Jageshwar Temple that enshrines the sacred Jyotir Lingam. The entrance is guarded by the 'dwarpals' (gate keepers) – the four armed Nandi is on the right while Bhrangi holding a three headed snake, is on the left. These dwarpals of Shiva guard the lingam that lies below a silver crown in the shape of a snake.

You now drive back to Almora and if spending the night here, you should stop at the Kasar Devi Temple, 7km short of town. This cave temple has

If you plan to spend the night at Binsar, you should leave the Jageshwar Temples by 4 p.m. so you get in before dark.

The climb to Kasar Devi takes only fifteen to twenty minutes and is worth making as this is the only cave temple in the region.

a rock inscription (dated second century BC), dedicated to the Goddess Kasar Devi who was worshipped by the early Kassites who settled here. In the late nineteeth century, Swami Vivekananda spent time here in meditation.

Almora is rather crowded and a stay here is not really recommended but if you do, we would suggest a delightful colonial home set in a clump of stately deodar trees. It is owned and run by the Wheeler family, old residents of Almora. The area near Kasar Devi Temple and the Crank's Ridge has

a choice of accommodation and is a recommended, though more expensive, place to stay. Kalmatia Sangam is probably the best option with its well-appointed individual cottages, international cuisine and even the chance of a relaxing massage or acupressure!

You could also drive out to Binsar, which has two or three places to choose from, and though further out, the forest here is enchanting.

Those heading back to Ranikhet will have to give Kasar Devi a miss due to time constraint ■

DAY 9
▸▸ Visit Binsar Forest and drive to Kausani

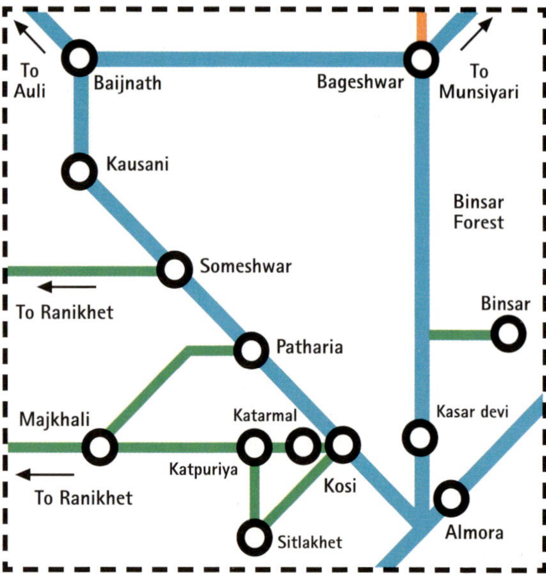

Binsar-Bageshwar	71 km	Kosi-Someshwar	24 km
Bageshwar-Baijnath	22 km	Someshwar-Kausani	11 km
Binsar-Kosi	44 km		

Don't worry about lunch as the KMVN rest house in Binsar turns out basic, but wholesome, fresh food.

This day of your journey starts with a walk in the enchanting Binsar Forest and then driving to Kausani. Although there is a shorter road to Kausani via Kosi River (50km), we recommend the longer (by 29km) route via Bageshwar. Since the Baijnath Temple complex is along this longer route, a stop here obviates the need to make a special 16km trip to it the next day.

Binsar (7900ft/2400m) was once the summer capital of the Chand Rajas. However, few traces remain of the ancient past other than the two thirteenth century temples dedicated to Shiva and Parvati. These lie in a meadow, 3km before the road ends.

Towering deodars in
the Binsar forest

Long tailed shrike

Binsar, also known as Bineshwar, witnessed a bit of revival as the seat of power between 1882 and 1886. Henry Ramsay was officially commissioner of Kumaon but behaved like its de facto king and built his residence and court at a vantage point on the hilltop here. He was fluent with the local Kumaoni dialect and rode from village to village dispensing justice. It is, however, fortunate that

If you are comfortable being on a vegetarian diet for a day or two, Khali Estate is the best place to stay — it is the only resort within Binsar Sanctuary.

the area received no further attention, as this is now one of the best preserved forests left in Kumaon. With its rich mixed forest of oak, rhododendron and deodar coupled with magnificent snow vistas stretching almost 300km across, any amount of time spent at Binsar seems inadequate!

In 1998, this area was declared a sanctuary and

In case you have had your fill of temples, give Bageshwar a miss and head straight for Kausani.

you have to pay an entry fee (Rs. 50 per vehicle and Rs. 10 per occupant), at the tollgate as you drive in. The road into the sanctuary has a reasonably good surface but is a narrow and steeply ascending one.

You should take a walk along one of the enchanting forest trails or head to the Forest Rest House, a kilometer or so beyond the KMVN. This marks the end of the track and is also a great viewpoint. Binsar is a bird watcher's paradise boasting over 150 species, including the khaleej pheasant. Although perfectly safe during the day, walking here in the dark is definitely avoidable; leopards and the Himalayan black bear frequent the area. In March/April, the rhododendrons are in full bloom and their vibrant colour against a

Baijnath Temples in the shadow of the snow capped mountains

Sculptures outside the main temple at Baijnath

backdrop of snowy mountains makes an indelible impression.

You could either carry a packed lunch and choose a beautiful spot to enjoy it or sample the basic but well cooked food at KMVN. However, do time yourself keeping in mind the 3-3.5 hours you need to get to Kausani, visiting the temples en route.

After soaking in the beauty of Binsar, you proceed to Kausani via Bageshwar, which stands at the confluence of the Saryu and Gomti rivers. The town is not particularly attractive but is an important pilgrim destination for Kumaonis as the ancient stone Baghnath Temple is located here. There is also the smaller Baneshwar Mahadev Temple (Mahadev represents Shiva as the Supreme Being, one who is both creator and destroyer). Despite its religious significance, this temple complex is in a state of disrepair and a short stop will suffice.

From here, the road leads down to the temple town of Baijnath (3700ft/1128m), home to a spectacular complex of temples along the West bank of the Gomti River. Comprising eighteen temples that date back to the twelfth century, the main one is in the center of the group and is dedicated to Shiva. It is adorned with numerous bells hung by devotees whose prayers for a son have been answered. The temple has carvings of various deities including Ganesh and Hanuman but the eye-catcher is the stunningly beautiful life-size statue of Parvati in the inner sanctum. This exquisite sculpture, (1.5m tall), has her holding many smaller carved images of Ganesh and shows Shiva astride Nandi, the bull. On the top left hand corner, a fantastic carving depicts the marriage of Shiva and Parvati which some believe took place at the confluence of the Gomti

Photography is not permitted inside the main temple but there is enough outside to keep shutterbugs happy!

Don't look for things to do in Kausani. You can even skip the twenty minute climb to the Anashakti Ashram and just enjoy the stunning views of the snowy mountains looming awesomely before you.

and Gorur Ganga rivers. Damaged during Aurangzeb's rule, only the lower part of the carving is original; the rest was restored in the nineteenth century using the original blocks. On the way out you can feed the fish in the nearby stream but tempted or not, remember catching them is prohibited!

There is also an old Vishnu temple at Kote ki Mai, 4km along the road to Gwaldam and the life-size statue of Vishnu here is meant to be a superb sculpture.

Kausani is only a 16km climb from Baijnath and lies on a ridge at 6200ft/1819m. On your way up you will encounter an unusual sight – slopes covered in tea bushes! Tea is grown in very limited parts of Kumaon and you should stop for a cuppa Kumaoni tea at the stall run by the Tea Board.

Kausani is famous for its brilliant snow views; all the more awesome for being much closer to them. Trishul, which represents Shiva's trident, is the predominant peak from Kausani and is only 50km away as the crow flies! You can see a 400km expanse of the Himalayas unfold before you; West to East are the peaks of Kedar, Chaukhamba, Badrinath, Nanda Ghunti, Trishul, Nanda Devi, Panchachuli and Api-Nampi in Nepal.

Mahatma Gandhi was enchanted by the views and beauty of Kausani and spent some time in 1929 at the Anashakti Ashram and christened this place the 'Switzerland of India'. Until her death recently, Sarlaben (aka Ms. Katherine Hellerman) managed the Anashakti Ashram. It continues to be a fully functional ashram. There is also a memorial-cum-museum of the noted Hindi litterateur Sumitra Nandan Pant at Kausani. However, in a nutshell, the three reasons you are in Kasauni are – 'for the view, the view and the view'!

Having reached Kausani, you now have a few options ahead of you and your choice will be dictated by both the amount of time on hand and your energy levels!

You can either spend a night at Corbett Park before returning to Delhi on the 11th day of your travel or, if you can spend another five to six days travelling, continue your 'Himalayan Odyssey' on to the important pilgrim destination of Badrinath and the spectacular region around it.

On the other hand, the flexibility of only three to four days and a spirit of adventure can lead you 'Off the Beaten Track' to the more remote but stunningly beautiful areas of Munsiyari, Dharchula, the Narayanswamy Ashram and Patal Bhuvaneshwar cave before returning via Pithoragarh to Ranikhet and on to Delhi ■

The Anashakti Ashram

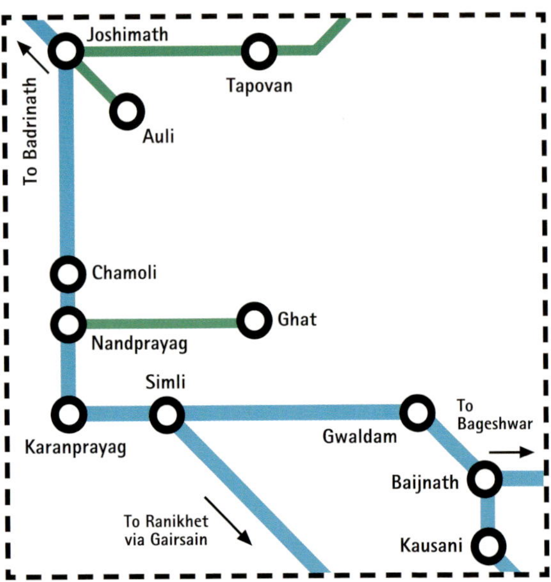

Kausani–Gwaldam	40 km		Chamoli–Joshimath	51 km
Gwaldam–Karanprayag	71 km		Joshimath–Auli	8 km
Karanprayag–Chamoli	31 km			

Landslides can be a hazard during the rainy season. Check if roads to Auli are open before heading out.

The second leg of your journey will take you to greater heights: Joshimath, Auli, Badrinath, and an optional visit to Tungnath and even Kedarnath.

From Kausani you backtrack 16km to Baijnath and then drive 24km to Gwaldam. When the views are clear you can see Trishul in all its magnificent glory from here. The road then descends to Karanprayag (one of the 'Panch Prayags') which marks the confluence of the Pindar and the Alaknanda rivers. You now ascend 20km to Nandprayag where the Nandakini joins the Alaknanda River. Chamoli, the district

headquarter, is 11km further but it is another
51km before you get to Joshimath
(6199ft/1890m). Auli is only 8km from Joshimath
but it is a steep climb up to its height –
9020ft/2750m. The drive from Karanprayag to
Joshimath is not very interesting – the rushing
Alaknanda being its only redeeming feature. In
addition, this section is prone to massive

You see a different aspect of Trishul from Gwaldam

landslides and if it has been raining recently you can expect delays. We do not recommend planning a journey on this road during the months of July to September.

Joshimath enjoys a pleasant climate and is a town with considerable religious significance but is otherwise a rather non-descript place. It is here that the ninth century philosopher and saint, Adi Shankaracharya of Kerala, spent time in meditation before embarking on his life's mission of reviving Hinduism as a faith. His initiative led to a rapid decline in the prevailing popularity of Buddhism and for the next four to five centuries

Heading for the meadows above Auli

Hinduism enjoyed a virtual monopoly in the religious aspects of life in this region.

As per legend, a 2500-year old cave that lies under a mulberry tree, a little above this town, is the place where the Adi Shankaracharya attained enlightenment. He established four 'Maths' (centers of learning), the first being the Jyotirmath at Joshimath. At the four cardinal points of the country, four 'dhams' (religious centers), were established — the first was at Badrinath, 31km further North. The other three dhams are at Rameshwaram in the South, Dwarka in the West and Puri in the East.

The most important of the temples at Joshimath is the Narsing Temple that depicts Vishnu in his half man-half lion incarnation. According to some, one of the arms of the idol is becoming thinner and will eventually fall off during the age of 'Kalyug'. The mighty Nar and Narayan mountains around Badrinath will then collapse, blocking the passage to the shrine, but the idols will reappear at Bhavishya Badri. There is already a small temple in place at this spot, around 18km from Joshimath, high up in the Tapovan valley. (If you have the time this is a beautiful place to visit — there are hot springs at Tapovan, but the temple is a 3km trek from the road)

Joshimath is not a great place to spend the night and you should aim to reach Auli before dark. Although a short distance (8km) away, the drive will take around half an hour as the road is narrow and steep. (If you are staying at Clifftop Club add another twenty minutes as the last 2km section to it is extremely rocky — a 'D-class' road!)

We do not advise you to attempt this section after dark as the chances of damaging your oil sump against large stones on the road are pretty high! ■

Since accommodation is extremely limited in Auli, call and book well in advance.

Remember you are at an altitude close to 10,000ft at Auli. Although you will be tempted to explore this beautiful place, take it easy and don't push yourself too much the first day.

DAYS 11 & 12
▸▸ Auli and around

Auli is perhaps one of the most pristine and beautiful spots in all of Uttarakhand. There is no human habitation close by and kudos should be given to those officials who decided to develop this as a ski resort. There is a 180° to 270° panoramic view of the Himalayas, with giants such as Nanda Devi, Trishul and Hathi Parbat lying only 10km away, as the crow flies. Above it is a dense forest of oak, rhododendron and deodar with gurgling streams rushing through and beyond the tree line lie the gently rolling bugyals (alpine meadows).

There are some great walks in this area but remember to take it easy as you are close to 10,000ft/3049m. One of these walks takes you through the forest, whereas the other is an uphill trek, past the last ski-lift tower, further into the bugyals.

In the monsoons, the bugyals spread out like a rich green carpet dotted with a multitude of brilliantly coloured wild flowers in vibrant contrast to the true blue skies and stunning white snow peaks. This is the first stage along the trekking route to Kuari Pass.

Fortunately Auli's claim to fame is that of a winter ski resort and since most of the summer tourist crowd has yet not 'discovered' it, you will probably find it quiet and peaceful!

There are only two places to stay: the up-market Clifftop Club that is accessed by a 4km un-metalled road and the GMVN complex that offers accommodation ranging from ordinary rooms to the better log cabins but is located at a lower height and does not command as spectacular and panoramic a view as Clifftop does.

In winter, depending on conditions, you may

have to park in Joshimath and take the 4km cable car ride to either of these places. The skiing season is generally between January and March but is dependant on the amount of snowfall. Courses for beginners are run by GMVN and are for a seven or fourteen day duration whereas private freelance instructors are available at Clifftop or near the slopes. Auli has so much to offer by way of natural beauty; so many wonderful walks and such a peaceful atmosphere that you could easily spend three, four or even more days here!

However, for our journey that is time bound, only within the covers of the book, after enjoying it all for two days, you move on to Badrinath — one of the holiest shrines a Hindu can visit ■

Hathi Parbat seen from Auli

DAYS 13 & 14
▸▸ Badrinath and around

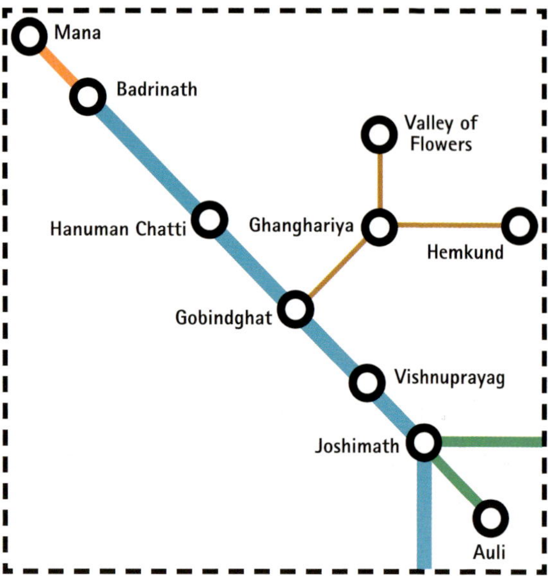

Carry a picnic lunch since you will probably want to get away from the crowds after visiting the popular shrine at Badrinath.

Auli-Gobindghat	29 km	Badrinath-Mana	3 km
Gobindghat-Badrinath	29 km		

The road from Joshimath to Badrinath is narrow but particularly scenic after Vishnuprayag (12km ahead), where the Alaknanda and Dhauli Ganga rivers meet. Sadly, even as you soak in these views, the ambience is ruined somewhat as you drive through a contrastingly scarred and dust-filled hillside – the work of a hydel project under construction. A jarring but evidently necessary note as hydel power is an otherwise non-polluting way of meeting energy needs and does not involve uprooting people as in the case of large dams. But given the fragile eco-system of the area and the frequent landslides it experiences, one can only hope the project has made a thorough study of the environmental impact and that this development does not prove more of a curse than a boon.

From Vishnuprayag it is 9km to Gobindghat, which is the base for treks to the Valley of Flowers and the Sikh pilgrim spot of Hemkund Sahib.

From Gobindghat the road ascends to Badrinath that lies at a height of 10,332ft/3150m. The town enjoys a magnificent setting with the giant, pyrammidical snow peak of Neelkanth (22,819ft/6957m), towering above, flanked by two other peaks; the Mana and Sunarsali. Below Neelkanth is the black mountain, Urvashi,

Sunset views from Auli

VALLEY OF FLOWERS AND HEMKUND SAHIB

This is a two to three day high altitude adventure, with the first stage taking you up to Ghangaria at 9971ft/3040m, which is the base camp for visiting either or both of these exotic locales. This 3936ft/1200m ascent is not easy and there are mules available at Gobindghat for those who do not want to slog it out (however, be prepared for some derisive looks from the pilgrims, young and old, climbing determinedly on the strength of their faith!)

According to Hindu mythology, during the battle with Ravana, Laxman was seriously wounded and barely alive when Ram deputed Hanuman to fly to the Himalayas in search of the 'Sanjivani Buti', a herb with miraculous healing properties. Flying all the way from Lanka, Hanuman scoured the length and breadth of the valley to find this herb but was confused by the huge array of plants and flowers. With his famed supernatural strength, he just scooped up the entire valley and carried it back to Ram!

Of the hundreds of varieties of flowers found in this valley, such as primulas, blue poppies, geraniums, campanulas are some rare specimens like the white androsace and many plants of medicinal value. The

flowers are on display in their full glory from mid–July to mid–August.

After spending the night in Ghangaria, in extremely basic accommodation, it is a gentle 4km climb to the U-shaped valley at 11,808ft/3600m. It is around six kilometers in length and two kilometers wide and has many streams weaving through it. If you are lucky, you will see a veritable carpet of flowers spread out in front

begun to choke the very same protected flowers out of existence.

The walk to Hemkund, at 14,199ft/4329m, is far more arduous and it is a steep six-kilometer climb. This high altitude lake with its icy-cold, brilliant blue waters is cradled in the lap of seven stately snow clad peaks — a sight that serves as a tonic to immediately dissipate your fatigue! The great Sikh guru, Guru Gobind Singh, is believed to have meditated here in a previous incarnation. There is a modern gurudwara with a daily 'langar' (meal kitchen), solicitously serving a hot meal to every faithful who has made it up here.

Hemkund is also known by the name 'Lokpal' and is a Hindu pilgrim site as well. It is here that Laxman meditated and regained his health after being wounded by Ravana's son Meghnath in the epic battle at Lanka. There is a small Laxman Temple adjacent to the gurudwara.

Strangely, despite its impressive historical antecedents, Hemkund was 'discovered' in 1930 by a Sikh soldier Hawaldar Sohan Singh and has developed as a major pilgrim destination only in the last fifty to sixty years.

of you. Popularised by the well known mountaineer Frank Smythe, in 1931, this valley has recently been declared a World Heritage Site and is also India's smallest national park. However, in recent years there has been some debate over the policy of closing the valley off to nomads who have traditionally grazed their livestock here. Apparently this grazing controlled a proliferating weed that now has

If you plan to spend the night here during the pilgrimage season, book accommodation well in advance if you don't want to end up in a crowded dharamsala!

connected by a saddle with the Narayan peak. Badrinath is aptly described in the ancient texts: "–there are many sacred spots in the heavens, earth and netherworld, but there is none equal to Badri and nor shall there be".

However, despite the superlative natural setting, the temple comes as a bit of a disappointment as it is located in the crowded main bazaar. It has none of the imposing stand-alone character of the temples at Kedarnath, Tungnath or Yamunotri. To reach it you cross the Alaknanda, which amazingly retains its fresh aqua colour even flowing through the town. On the West bank is the brightly painted, albeit slightly garish, hive-shaped shrine. Avalanches have destroyed the temple several times in the past and the present structure is around two centuries old. The past history of the temple is not clear but it is believed to have been an important center of pilgrimage in the Vedic age (1500-1200 BC). It was converted into a Buddhist shrine during Ashoka's reign in the third century BC. The Adi Shankaracharya, after attaining enlightenment at Joshimath, proceeded to Badrinath and in a dream was instructed to retrieve the 'shaligram' (black stone), idol of the temple. This had been secreted in the Narad Kund by priests to protect it from destruction by unknown, or unnamed, iconoclastic forces.

Just below the temple complex is the 'Tapt Kund' (hot springs), in whose sulphur waters one is supposed to take a dip before entering the temple. There are five sacred blocks of stone around the Tapt Kund which are known as the 'Panch Shilas'. These are named after the various sages who, in the distant past, meditated on them. Between the Tapt and Narad Kund stands the conical 'Naradshila'. Below this, in the waters of the

Alaknanda is the 'Narsingshila'. After slaying the demon king Hiranyakashyap, Vishnu (in his nar-sing – 'man-lion', avatar) entered the icy waters to soothe his temper and liking the spot remained here till his body became the shila. The lion-shaped rock with its gaping jaw and hooked claws is best viewed from the opposite bank. The 'Barahshila' is also in the river and it is the petrified incarnation of Vishnu as a boar, with his faithful 'vehicle', the Garur, lying nearby as the 'Garurshila'. The last of the shilas is the one occupied by the sage Markandey who attained 'param-shanti' (eternal peace), with the blessings of Sri Badrinathji and this is the 'Markandeyshila' which is barely visible in the waters of the Alaknanda.

The Vishnu Temple at Badrinath

LORD VISHNU AT BADRINATH

As per Hindu mythology, Vishnu was resting on his 'sesha shaya' (his serpentine throne), on the Kshir-sagar (celestial ocean), with his consort the Goddess Laxmi gently massaging his feet. Narad Muni, a sage of the highest repute but known for stirring things up, was passing by and chided Vishnu for his un-godlike behavior. Vishnu was abashed and sent Laxmi to the nag-kanyas (attendant serpent-women) while he himself descended to the Himalayan valley now known as Badrinath to do penance. This valley has an abundant growth of 'badri', a type of wild berry, that gave Vishnu sustenance while he was in penance; hence the name Badrinath. Vishnu assumed a 'yog-dhyani' posture and went into deep meditation for several years. During this time, Laxmi searched the heavens high and low and then finally came down to earth and found him in this mountain retreat. She implored him to return to his original 'sringaric' form. Acceding to her request, he laid down three conditions to be followed by all visitors to this region: the valley was to remain a place of meditation and not for worldly pleasures; that he would be worshipped in both forms — the Gods would worship him in the yog-dhyani form, while humans would do so in the sringaric form; and lastly, Laxmi would sit on his right side in the sringaric form and on the left in the yog-dhyani form. Traditionally, as his wife, Laxmi would be seen seated on his left but here they are worshipped as two separate divine entities and not as a divine couple. For this reason the 'rawal' (pujari), of Badrinath is always a bachelor. In summer, when the temple is open Vishnu is worshipped in his sringaric form while in winter when the idols are brought down and are not for public viewing, Laxmi's position is reversed for 'darshan' by sages and the gods.

The temple is generally open from mid–May to mid–November and the head priest is still chosen from the Shankaracharya's Namboodri community of Kerala Brahmins. The closure of the temple involves an elaborate ceremony when the Vishnu shaligram is draped with a 'choli' especially woven by girls of the Molapa families who reside in nearby Mana village. Vishnu and the other temple deities are then shifted to Pandukeshwar, 21km before Badrinath, to protect their loss or damage in the event of an avalanche or any such natural calamity.

AROUND BADRINATH

If you have not made an early start, the 'gate system' of traffic control is likely to get you! This regulates movement of traffic in one direction at a time and you need to ascertain the timings from Joshimath before starting or else you may end up parked on the roadside for three hours! If you have made it through the first gate or are planning to spend the night at Badrinath, there are a couple of walking excursions nearby that you could choose to undertake. Depending on the time available you could even squeeze in a visit to both, if you so desire.

A 3km drive brings you to the village of Mana, the last habitation before the border with Tibet, which lies only 30km away. This village is inhabited by Bhotiyas who were originally nomads from Tibet. Prior to the war with China in 1962, these Bhotiyas made their living trading goods across the high passes into Tibet. The trading has now been replaced by animal husbandry, some limited cultivation and many are now engaged in weaving pure wool durries using traditional Tibetan designs.

A short 200m walk brings you to the Vyas Gufa

In case you are making a day excursion to Badrinath and have a few hours to spare, drive to Mana village and walk up to Vasundhara Falls.

(cave), where the legendary author of the *Mahabharat* is believed to have dictated his epic to Lord Ganesh. You can cross the river using the Bhim Pul (bridge), which was built single-handedly by Bhim, the strongman of the Pandava clan, to enable his brothers make their way across. A further 4km walk brings you to the base of the Vasundhara Falls, believed by many to be the source of the Alaknanda as it falls from heaven.

With a good guide and a strong pair of legs, you can trek and explore the beautiful and myth-laden area beyond Vasundhara Falls. Make an early start so you can return by mid-afternoon.

BEYOND THE VASUNDHARA FALLS

You will have to slot a whole day for this excursion and should definitely engage the services of a guide.

A 4km trek brings you to a grove of trees that seem to suddenly come up on you in this rocky, barren countryside. This spot is known as Laxmi Van, as the goddess is believed to have meditated here. Yet another 3km takes you to the Alkapuri Glacier and the Alaknanda River emerges from as many as five snouts of this glacier. The views of Neelkanth and Chaukhamba peaks, and the Alaknanda emerging from the glacier, make an awesome sight. Chakrateerth is a lovely meadow 6km ahead where the Nar and Narayan mountains meet to form a circular valley. From here a walk of 4km brings you to Satopanth Lake that lies at 14,452ft/4406m. This astoundingly triangular shaped lake is believed to be the place where Brahma, Vishnu and Shiva meditated at the three corners. Supposed to be an earthly replica of the Kshir-sagar, this pristine, crystal clear lake is bewitchingly beautiful. The Swargarohini peak (Stairway to Heaven) lies ahead and its seven ridges are arranged like steps that the Pandavas are supposed to have taken on their journey to heaven.

Another shorter and more do-able trek from Mana takes you 3km along the ancient trade route to Tibet. Here you can see the legendary Saraswati River emerge from a lateral glacier. It was with the blessings of this goddess of learning that Vyas

Amaranthus plants pepper the cultivated fields

was able to compose the *Mahabharat* at Mana. Flowing past the Vyas Gufa, it merges with the Alaknanda at Keshavprayag. If one is to believe legend, it then flows underground to the Prayagraj near Allahabad, remaining unseen even at its confluence there with the Ganga and Yamuna.

Yet another excursion that you could make involves a bit of climbing and starts just behind the main Badrinath Temple. There are two paths here and one of these is a thirty-minute ascent to Chandrapaduka, where a boulder bears an impression believed to be Vishnu's footprint. The other path takes you to Bamni village, only a kilometer away. Just above the village is a small temple dedicated to Urvashi, the beautiful nymph deployed by Indra to try and distract the sage Arghya while he was meditating. You then head back to your aerie at Auli as the next day involves an early start and a lot of driving ■

Nanda Devi from above Auli

▸▸ Auli to Ranikhet via Adibadri (225km) and on to Delhi

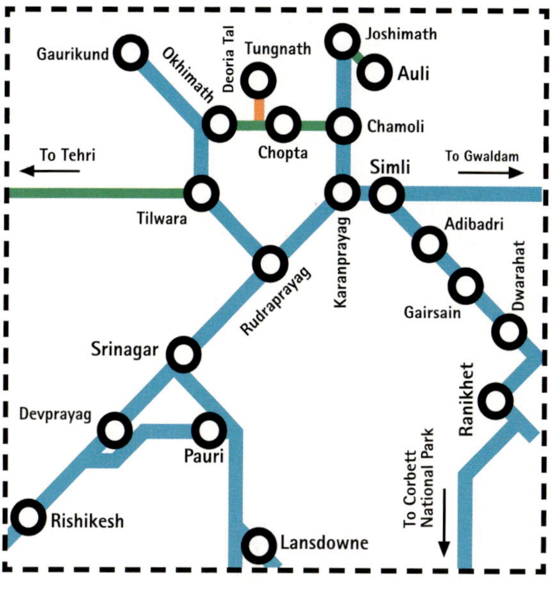

The route we are recommending is different from the one you took on the way out. If you want to stick with the 'Old Faithful', head towards Gwaldam and then onto Ranikhet.

Auli-Chamoli	59 km	Gairsain-Dwarahat	57 km
Chamoli-Simli	37 km	Dwarahat-Ranikhet	32 km
Simli-Gairsain	40 km		

If you are planning to visit Corbett National Park on your return, (only open between November 15 and June 15), your route will take you back to Ranikhet for the night. Retrace your tracks up to Karanprayag and from there, instead of going to Gwaldam, turn right at Simli, 6km from Karanprayag. This less travelled route goes past Adibadri, 11km from the turn off. There is an ancient temple complex here that dates back to the Gupta period and the Narayan Temple has a magnificent three-foot tall black stone image of Vishnu. You then ascend to Gairsain, 27km ahead,

and down to Dwarahat that is 57km further. Ranikhet is a 32km climb from here and we estimate you should allow eight to ten hours for this journey.

On the last and sixteenth day you can return to Delhi either directly or with a stop at Corbett Park ■

Preparing for the evening 'aarti' on the banks of the Ganga at Rishikesh

▸▸ To Rishikesh or Tungnath and Okhimath

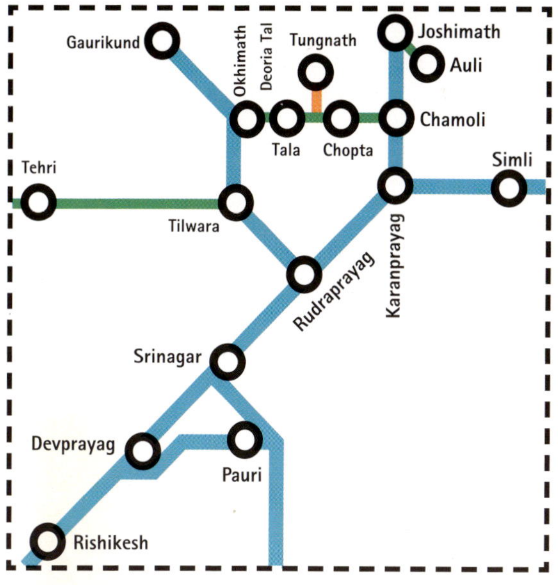

The drive to Rishikesh is mostly at low altitudes and during the summer is not a very pleasant one.

Auli-Chamoli	59 km	Tala-Okhimath	22 km
Chamoli-Chopta	50 km	Okhimath-Gaurikund	45 km
Chopta-Tala	15 km		

In the event you decide to take the alternate route and are heading back via Rishikesh, the road takes you to Karanprayag (90km) after which you drive along the Alaknanda River all the way till you reach Devprayag. Around 32km along this section of the drive you pass Rudraprayag, where the Mandakini joins the Alaknanda, and just 5km short of this town, look out for a sign marking the spot where Jim Corbett killed the infamous man-eater of Rudraprayag. With terraced fields all around you, it is difficult to imagine that this entire area was once a thick jungle abounding in wild life and with very little human habitation! It is a 70km drive from Rudraprayag to Devprayag (with Srinagar lying almost half way along the route) and is another 68km further to Rishikesh town. However, if you are planning on rafting the next day, remember most of these camps are by the riverbank, 15km short of town. Since some sections of the road between Karanprayag and Devprayag are quite flat, this drive of 258km can be negotiated in 8-10 hours.

Yet another option that is open to you on this route is to turn right at Chamoli (51km from Joshimath), for Gopeshwar. You can then drive 50km through excellent variegated forest to Chopta (8856ft/2700m), which is the base for the climb up to the temple at Tungnath. In spring this drive is absolutely breathtaking as the rhododendrons are in bloom and there are more shades of pink here than you thought possible! Other species of trees complement the colour palette with greens ranging from the fresh 'new-green' leaves to deep rich olive tones — an enchanting riot of colour with dappled light playing patterns on it.

The only accommodation available on this diversion to Tungnath and Okhimath is the network of KMVN Rest Houses.

The temple is only 3.5km from the road but it is a steep climb up to 12,070ft/3680m and will take at least two hours. During the tourist season mules may be available at Chopta. Tungnath holds special significance, as it is one of the 'Panch Kedars'. This stone temple, with a Nandi bull in front, is a comparatively simple structure but is considered one of the most venerated of Hindu shrines in the country.

Another 1.5km along the track will bring you to the Chandrashila peak, 12,890ft/3930m, which offers an unobstructed view of the solid, fortress-like Chaukhamba peak as well as several others like Neelkanth, Kedarnath and Nanda Devi.

After coming down from Tungnath, you drive approximately 15km to Tala and then on to

After the passions raised during the epic war of Mahabharata settled, came the time for atonement. The Pandavas sought pardon from Shiva for having killed their kinsmen and even gurus, who had been by their side and guided them through their youth. They travelled to Kashi and sought an audience with Shiva. However, he was in no mood to oblige them and went to the Himalayas where he lived incognito at Guptkashi (near Okhimath), thus giving this place its name. The Pandavas, who were now completely overwhelmed

Kedarnath Temple

with remorse, did not give up and traced him to his hiding place. Shiva then transformed himself into a bull and joined a herd of cows grazing peacefully on the lush hillsides. Bhim, the strongest of the Pandava brothers, was the only one to see through this disguise. Straddling two peaks, he allowed the herd to pass between his legs and as Shiva approached he reached down to hold him back. Shiva, however, dived underground, leaving only his rump for Bhim to clutch on to. Impressed by the perseverance and genuine remorse of the Pandavas, Shiva emerged and finally granted them his 'darshan', exonerating them from their sins.

The five places where the various parts of Shiva's body emerged are known as the Panch Kedars. These are Tungnath for the arms (bahu), Rudranath for the face (mukh), Madhya Maheshwar for the stomach (nabi) and Kalpeshwar for the hair (jata). Kedarnath, where the rear part of his body emerged is considered the most sacred of all and following Shiva's instructions to worship the rump, the Pandavas constructed a temple here. According to the Puranas, the front potion of his body emerged at Pashupatinath in Kathmandu (Nepal).

JOURNEY TO KEDARNATH

(A drive of 45km from Okhimath to Gaurikund and a 14km trek up to the Kedarnath Temple)

The road takes you to Guptkashi where Shiva lived incognito while trying to avoid being tracked down by the Pandava brothers. You then pass through Rampur on to Sonprayag from where you can take a 5km detour to visit Triyuginarayan. This village has a temple dedicated to Vishnu who presided over the legendary wedding between Shiva and Parvati that is believed to have been held here. The sacred fire in front of the temple is supposed to have been alight ever since this divine union took place. You can then drive to Gaurikund (6498ft/1981m), the last motorable point before the arduous 14km (5-6 hours) climb to the temple. It is at Gaurikund that Parvati engaged in several centuries of meditation to impress Shiva with her devotion and persuade him to end the state of splendid isolation he had retreated to while mourning the death of his consort, Sati. Once Shiva finally agreed to come out of this state and marry her, Parvati came to be worshipped as Gauri and Shiva as Mahadev in an ancient temple here.

The Kedarnath Temple is in the most spectacular setting that takes your breath away and the entire fatigue of the trek up is very quickly forgotten!

The Kedarnath peak (22,304ft/6800m), dominates the sky scape behind the shrine and the gigantic snow mountains looming overhead provide an awesome background to this temple. The glacier behind the temple is the source of the Mandakini River that emerges as three streams and is joined by a fourth before cascading down the mountainside like a waterfall. An enduring and powerful visual memory is one of this temple at dusk — silhouetted darkly against an ink-blue sky, with the last light still on the snow peaks, and the rich evocative ochre of the pandit's robes with the bright orange flame as he did the evening 'aarti' to the Nandi in the courtyard.

Within the inner sanctum the main object of devotion is the large black conical stone representing the rump of the bull, or Shiva himself, making this the most important of the Panch Kedars. Kedarnath is also regarded as one of the twelve Jyotir Lingams; thus this shrine is doubly sacred and important. The courtyard has a large stone Nandi bull; Lord Shiva's 'dwarpals', Jai and Vijay, guard the doorway and the outer chamber walls have sculptures of the five Pandavas and Draupadi. The rear of the temple has the Samadhi of Adi Shankaracharya marked by a giant fist holding a staff. There are coloured flags at the site of a Bhairon Temple. Bhairon is the guardian deity of Kedarnath during the winter.

Okhimath, 22km further. There is a possible
diversion that you can take from Tala – there is a
2km track starting from Saari village to Deoria Tal
(7997ft/2438m), a beautiful high altitude lake
ringed by snowy mountains.

Okhimath is the winter seat of the gods from
Kedarnath, Rudranath and Madhya Maheshwar
and this is where you can make a well earned
night halt. This also serves as a base if you are
planning to include Kedarnath in your list of
places to visit ■

Tungnath Temple

The holy confluence of the
Bhagirathi and Alaknanda at
Devprayag

▸▸ To Rishikesh or Ranikhet

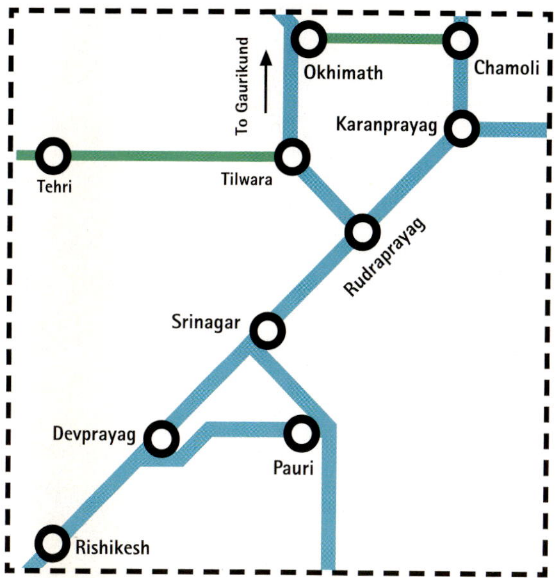

Okhimath-Rudraprayag	39 km	Srinagar- Devprayag	35 km
Rudraprayag-Karanprayag	32 km	Devprayag-Rishikesh	68 km
Rudraprayag-Srinagar	34 km		

Traffic on the Delhi-Haridwar road is diverted end July-early August every year, when the 'kanwarias', carrying their precious cargo of 'Ganga jal', are given the right of way.

From Okhimath you drive down to Rudraprayag with a possible stop at Nala where there is a Buddhist shrine; the only remnant of this religion in the area. From Rudraprayag, you drive on to Rishikesh on the road described earlier, or come back to Karanprayag and on to Ranikhet for the night. If you want to visit and explore Rishikesh and Haridwar, you will need an extra day or two. Relaxing by the river or rafting down it would be a great way to end your holiday if you have had enough of sightseeing. Details of this area are in 'From the Other End of the Spectrum'.

The eighteenth and final day of your journey takes you back to Delhi ■

OPTION **2** – SHORT 'N' SWEET
DAY 10

OPTION **2** – SHORT 'N' SWEET
DAY 10
▶▶ **To Corbett National Park**

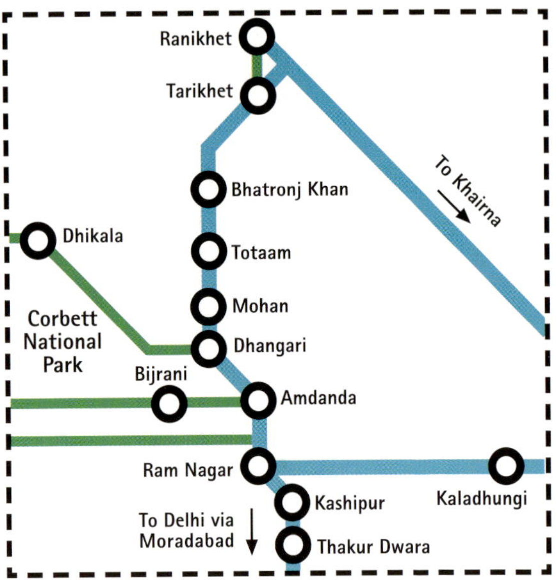

Even if you aren't stopping at the Park, the alternate route from Ranikhet, via Corbett, is worth taking. It is curvaceous but scenic and well forested. Check road conditions if driving post-monsoons.

Ranikhet- Bhatronjkhan	27 km	Ramnagar-Kashipur	26 km
Bhatronjkhan-Mohan	44 km	Kashipur-Moradabad	
Mohan-Ramnagar	25 km	(by-pass)	48 km

If time has run out and you have to head back home, we recommend an interesting diversion on your return journey. You drive back to Ranikhet next morning and via Tarikhet head down to Corbett National Park for the night. This route out of Ranikhet is less frequented and though the surface is good, the road is narrow and twists through pine forests all the way to the foothills at Mohan (unlike the more barren approach you made coming in). Although the distance to the entrance of the park is 80km, you should factor in 3 hours for the journey. After the rains, there are some bad sections where the water runs through,

ripping the road surface and also bringing in
rocks and stones and in this season you should
check road conditions before starting the drive.

Once you get there, settle into your hotel room
and then go out for an evening 'ghoom' (drive) to
the forest – you could get lucky and sight the
majestic tiger and that would certainly be a more
than perfect end to your exciting holiday!

This park is India's first National Park and was
established in 1936. Originally named after Sir
Malcolm Hailey, the then governor of the United
Provinces, it was renamed the Ram Ganga
National Park after Independence and ten years
later, in 1957, was rechristened Corbett National
Park after the legendary Jim Corbett.

Corbett National Park is located in the Shivalik
foothills of the mighty Himalayas and covers

Hathi mera saathi!

Crossing the Ramganga

521sq.km. It is set in dense, predominantly 'sal' forest in the Patlidev valley that the Ram Ganga River traverses.

The Patlidev valley was originally heavily forested but since it was located on the border between Garhwal and the Rohilla kingdom, territorial disputes led to vast areas of land being cleared so the Garhwali army could set up encampments. Following the Gorkha invasion and the subsequent treaty with the British, this region fell into the hands of the Garhwalis. The large valley, sans the original forest cover, remained uninhabited resulting in the emergence of grasslands (chaur). Combined with the remaining forests that border these grasslands, this became the ideal habitat for elephant, tiger, deer and other large wildlife.

Today, Corbett Park is one of the best National

Parks in the country and definitely worth a visit even if your interest in wildlife is minimal. For nature lovers, there is a veritable bounty of flora and fauna to be experienced at close quarters. The forest is dominated by handsome 'sal' trees that grow to heights of 35m and allow several layers of vegetation to grow under, or alongside them. This park's eco system includes a wide variety of trees, shrubs, climbers, fungi and lichens. There is another distinct eco system near the rivers and streams consisting of 'Khair' and 'Sissu' (teak) trees that grow in sandy, gravelly exposed ground; their roots add nitrogen to the soil, improving fertility and thus helping other advantageous species of vegetation to grow. Once this whole eco-cycle culminates, the land is rich enough for the 'sal' trees — this 'sal' forest could take centuries to come up! (A realisation that makes you wish you never see a 'sal' tree cut down!)

Don't be surprised if the resident wildlife at Dhikala wanders on to the verandah outside your room!

The 'Khair-Sissu' forest provides shelter and cover for the deer, its predators as also nesting space for birds.

The 'chaur', which are savannah-like grasslands, are favoured by elephant, deer and this is where the tiger comes to hunt and can be spotted if you are at the right place at the right time — in other words, if you are in luck! Every winter a careful exercise of controlled burning is undertaken and that leads to fresh growth of grass for the deer and other grazers to feed on.

The park is home to 50 varieties of mammals, 100 species of birds and 25 kinds of reptiles. At the southern of the park, construction of a dam has lead to the creation of the Ram Ganga reservoir, now home to many species of waterfowl.

While staying in the Park, forays into the jungle are scheduled in the early mornings and in the evenings. One has the option of taking an elephant

JIM CORBETT

Jim Corbett was born in Nainital in 1875 and in his childhood developed a fascination for the jungles that almost hemmed Nainital at that time. He developed a keen under-standing of, and sensitivity to, the workings of these eco systems.

As was the fashion in that era, he learnt to shoot and soon became a crack shot. His first big game kill was a leopard, shot at the tender age of eight! As he grew older, the tiger became his preferred prey. One naturally wonders how this park (also the first to be included in the ambitious Project Tiger to preserve the species), was named after a person who missed the century mark in tiger-kills by a mere whisker! The answer lies in the pages of history — from the early ages hunting has been part of man's genetic make up. As civilisation grew, it became a major sport and a symbol of strength and valour that brought instant social status with it. What is taboo today, and indeed a grave criminal act, was the norm and preferred sport in yesteryears.

In India, once the agrarian society developed, hunting ceased to be a need and soon became the preserve of the ruling class. Many a reputation was made or lost depending on the person's hunting prowess. Certainly till Independence and probably for some time thereafter, the standing of the male scion of a royal family was measured less by his shooting ability on the range and more by the number and size of his 'kills' in 'shikar' (hunt).

Jim Corbett lived most of his life being part of this world, but gave up shooting for pleasure in the mid 1920s because he recognised the threat of extinction faced by various species of wild life. He was therefore considered by many to be one of the first conservationists and was one of the main moving forces behind the establishment of this park.

This is not to say that he completely gave up the gun — he now killed only those leopards and tigers that had deviated from seeking their natural prey and had turned into man-eaters. Shooting these dreaded man-eaters, he soon became a hero for the local population as many villages in the Kumaon foothills were densely forested and under threat at that time.

He wrote books on his exploits and they were not only immensely popular but the tales have passed into lore in many instances. *Man Eaters of Kumaon*, *Jungle Lore* and *Man-eating Leopard of Rudraprayag* are just a few of his well-known books.

Elephants crossing the 'chaur' in Corbett Park

ride or driving along the narrow forest tracks. In both cases, a forest guide will accompany you. There is a virtual guarantee that you will sight deer of four varieties – the 'chital' (spotted deer), the majestic 'sambar', the barking deer and the diminutive hog deer. You are also likely to spot wild boar and wild elephants lurking in the shadows. Crocodiles and 'Gharials' sunning themselves on the banks of the river can be seen from a vantage point. The elusive tiger may not grant you a 'darshan' but between April and June, the chances of sighting increase as the animal can be seen heading for water holes or streams as also for salt licks, besides his usual haunts.

The park is open from November 15th to June 15th and we strongly recommend staying at Dhikala, the Government Tourist Complex located in the core of the park area. The accommodation is simple and not even close to that provided in the many luxurious private hotels along the main road outside the park. However, this is where the action is and if you are planning on spending some time here, surrendering creature comforts for a night or two will pay back in some memorable experiences. Another option within the park is the three-room rest house at Khinnanauli but you need to make reservations well in advance for this place.

Staying outside entails visiting the park through the Amdanda Gate and being limited to the area around Bijrani, which is a poorer option to Dhikala in terms of the wealth of fauna you could possibly see. However you can still tour the Dhikala region by booking yourself on one of the two available canters. A third gate has also recently been opened at Jhirni. (N.B: For bookings, one needs to contact the Director, Corbett Tiger Reserve, Ram Nagar-244715 (Nainital) Tel: 05947-251489; Fax: 251376 – or the Dehradun office at 85, Rajpur Road; Tel: 0135-2744225. Bookings can also be made through the KMVN or GMVN offices in Delhi).

If you cannot stop at Corbett this trip, remember it is only a four to five hour drive from Delhi and ideal for a weekend break.

FISHING

This area is an angler's delight and fishing is permitted outside the boundaries of the National Park. The director, Corbett Tiger Reserve issues permits for use in the Kosi, Ram Ganga, Mandal and Kothri rivers. The fishing season begins on October 15th and ends on June 30th.

CORBETT MUSEUM

A short drive from Ram Nagar brings you to Kaladhungi where there is a museum dedicated to Jim Corbett. En route you pass a small waterfall and Kaladhungi is the starting point for an extremely scenic forest drive to Nainital ■

OPTION **3** – 'OFF THE BEATEN TRACK'
"Two roads diverged in a wood, and I –
I took the one less traveled by,
And that has made all the difference".
— *Robert Frost*

DAY 10
▸▸ **Drive to Chaukori. Visit Patal Bhuvaneshwar & Gangolighat**

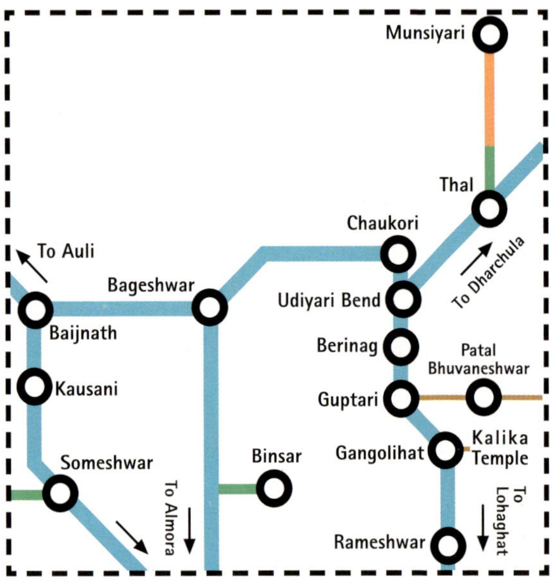

From Bageshwar the drive is through thick forest on a narrow ascending road. The surface is by and large good but progress will be on the slower side.

Kausani-Bageshwar	38 km	Chaukori-Thal	25 km
Bageshwar-Chaukori	46 km	Thal-Munsiyari	74 km
Chaukori-Berinag	10 km	Thal-Dharchula	85 km
Berinag- Patal Bhuvaneshwar	29 km		

Make a reasonably early start from Kausani and retrace your tracks up to Bageshwar (38km), and then turn right on the road going to Chaukori. The distance to be covered is 84km and will take around three hours. There is a good KMVN tourist complex here and Chaukori is famous for its view of the Panchachuli peaks. Stop for a quick cup of 'chai' if you want, before proceeding to Berinag and on to Patal Bhuvaneshwar Cave (around 40km). The drive is an enjoyable one, through dense forest. Once you get there, park your car and take the longer walk through the village — there is an old stone mandir here, set in a courtyard and on the 'shikhar' of the temple is an interesting, almost primitive depiction of Lord Shiva. Closeby is a room containing a number of

A primitive image of Shiva on the temple at Patal Bhuvaneshwar village

small and large statues, unearthed in this area.

Beyond the village, just under an overhanging rock face, is the entrance to the Patal (meaning 'underground') Bhuvaneshwar Cave. There is an entrance fee to be paid and a local temple committee regulates the numbers going in. Photography is not allowed and cameras are to be deposited at this point. This is a natural cave carved out of lime rock as a result of water erosion. The entrance is narrow and tunnel-like with the rocks 'polished' to a slippery smoothness by the people sliding down them. There are strong metal chains to hold but don't even think of giving it a try if you are even mildly claustrophobic! Once you reach the floor of the cave, there is standing room and it is reasonably lit. At the 'entrance chamber' you get a sense of how huge the cave really is and there are passageways leading to other 'chambers' and sections. The floor is slippery with water and you

'Shiva's Jatta', underground in the Patal Bhuvaneshwar Cave

need to tread carefully. There are fascinating
stalactite and stalagmite formations everywhere
and the guide points out specific formations with
a torch, explaining which facets of the shape
identifies it as a particular god. There are lime
formations water-sculpted into the shape of Shesh
Nag, Ganesh, Badrinath, Kedarnath, Garur, and of
course the Jyotir Lingams. It takes a religiously
inclined person, with a fanciful imagination, to
'recognise' these forms. However, irrespective of
imagery, these formations are fascinating and the
sheer extent of the cave awesome. Particularly
striking is the 'Shiva's Jatta' (locks) – with
'corded' limestone running down a rock face and
the play of light on water sliding down its ridges
– it is truly an amazing sight.

Local legend holds that this cave is connected by
an underground passage to Mt. Kailash and the
other end exits at Rameshwaram Ghat at the
confluence of Kali, Ram Ganga and Saryu. Lord
Shiva is believed to have used this passage.

Your visit to the cave can take an hour and there
are only a few dhabas here with very little on
offer by way of lunch – Patal Bhuvaneshwar has
not yet been 'discovered'! The Parvati Resort, 3km
before the cave, provides decent food and
accommodation. If you have had enough driving
for the day, you could even decide to spend the
night here. This would however add an extra hour
and half to the next day's drive of 4-5 hours and
hence we recommend returning to Chaukori.

For those still in the mood for more sightseeing,
on your way back when the side road to Patal hits
the Chaukori road, take the opposite direction
from Chaukori. A 6km drive brings you to
Gangolighat. The Hat Kalika temple here is
ascribed to Adi Shankaracharya and is one of the
108 Shakti Peeths. Located in a grove of deodars,

Consider carrying a
packed lunch as Patal
Bhuvaneshwar has very
little to offer in terms of
food, unless you stop at
Parvati Resort.

A hillside shrine

this temple was built fifty years ago and enlarged during later renovations. There are several temples and caves, including a sun temple, within a 5km-walking radius of Gangolighat. There may be some who are not inclined to burrow underground and prefer to do their sightseeing from terra firma. If so, you could actually look around Chaukori and proceed directly to Munsiyari but do remember to carry a packed lunch if you are taking this option. Around 4km out of Chaukori, at the Udiyari Bend, turn left for Thal (21km further). Just beyond Thal you turn left again for Munsiyari. With this last section of around 74km being an uphill drive on not very good roads, it will take 3-4 hours to negotiate ■

⏩ Drive to Munsiyari

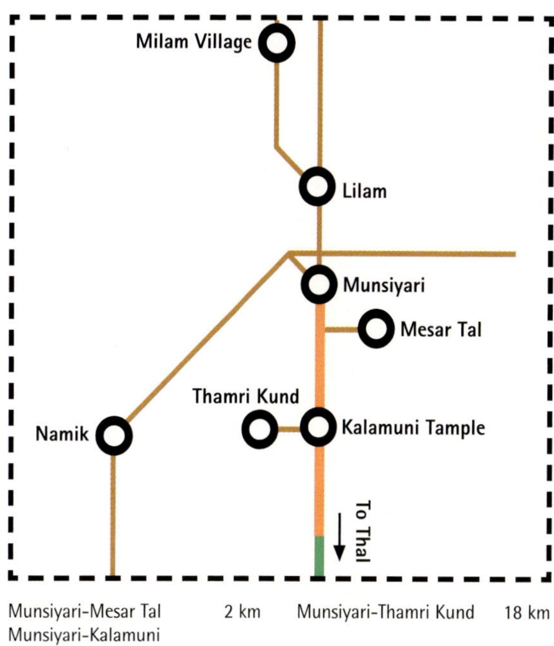

Munsiyari-Mesar Tal	2 km	Munsiyari-Thamri Kund	18 km
Munsiyari-Kalamuni Temple	16 km		

Munsiyari has developed a facet of eco-tourism — village homes now offer one to two rooms with toilet facilities to tourists. The cost is approximately Rs. 300/- per night including meals!

Munsiyari, at 7600ft/2317m, is a quiet town that enjoys unparalleled views of the five majestic Panchachuli peaks. According to local lore, the peaks served as the five 'chulas' (fires or stoves) used to cook the Pandava's last meal before they left for heaven and these 'chulas' froze in time!

You can stop and visit Kalamuni Temple that lies just as you crest the last hill before descending somewhat to Munsiyari. The hillside around Kalamuni is gently sloping and covered in grasses and tiny wild flowers in the monsoon and in winter is covered in snow and could be ideal for short ski runs. Another place to visit is Mesar Tal that lies above an old oak and rhododendron

The five peaks of Panchachuli seen from Munsiyari

forest. With hardly a soul in sight, ringed by lichen and moss covered trees and with only the loud persistent sound of cicadas in hearing, this lake seems locked in time! Actually Munsiyari is a nice place to spend time in – besides the incredible snow views there are great forest walks and some 'bugyals' (alpine meadows), at easy trekking distance. It is the base for treks to the Milam, Ralam and Namik glaciers, Thamari Kund and of course for mountaineers heading for Panchachuli ■

▸▸ Visit Narayanswamy Ashram and stay at Dharchula

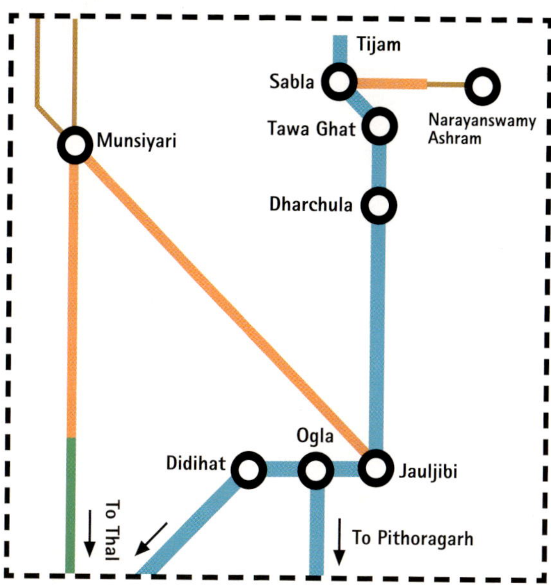

Munsiyari-Jauljibi	60 km	Tawa Ghat-Narayanswamy	
Jauljibi-Dharchula	27 km	Ashram	25 km
Dharchula-Tawa Ghat	19 km		

If, perchance, you end up spending a night at the Ashram, besides the peace and tranquility you may enjoy great views of the Nepal Himalayas.

The next day calls for an early start and a fair bit of driving. The first leg of 60km brings us way down to Jauljibi on the banks of the Dhauli Ganga River that serves as a border with Nepal. You can cross the river by a footbridge if you want. This leg of the journey will take around two hours and from here you drive past Dharchula (27km) to Tawa Ghat, 19km further. You turn left from Tawa Ghat, past the dam under construction, and drive 8km along a rough road to Sabla where you cross the river. The next 17km is a rather dramatic drive, climbing from around 3000ft/915m to 6000ft/1829m on a dirt track

The Narayanswamy Ashram

specially designed to test the suspension of your vehicle! We recommend hiring a jeep from Dharchula for this 88km journey to and back from the ashram. The rate will depend on your negotiating skills but something between Rs. 1000 to Rs.1500 for a full vehicle would be a good deal. The drive is certainly spine tingling and not for the faint hearted, with a sheer drop of almost 3000ft on one side as you ascend! It is, however, well worth making the effort as the ashram, at 8971ft/2735m, is located in a beautiful, serene setting and the building is particularly unique in its architecture.

The ashram serves a hot lunch to visitors if you

are there at the time and if you strike the right
chord, they will even accommodate you for the
night. However, assuming you decide to head
back, Dharchula is the nearest option for a night
halt. Dharchula is a regular large township and
the KMVN bungalow is at a vantage point along
the Kali Ganga River and although just another
modern construction, it has a great sit out
overlooking the river and the food is good. You
can actually walk across a footbridge into Nepal
from town.

Your other option is to drive another 58km
(approximately two hours), to the cooler heights
of the KMVN at Didihat ■

Peeping into Nepal!

NARAYANSWAMY ASHRAM

The founder Raghvendra was born on 'Dattatreya Jayanti' in 1908 in distant Mangalore on the Karnataka coast. The family were Saraswat brahmins and Raghvendra grew up in an environment where 'bhajans' and 'kirtans' were performed regularly. The sudden death of his father, while he was still a teenager, compelled the family to move to Rangoon where his uncle worked as a district forest official. Raghvendra spent much of his time reading the scriptures and was influenced by the writings of Swami Vivekanand, S. Ram Tirath and Ramakrishna Paramhans' Kathamrit. His mother was not happy with these developments and he was sent to Karachi to study engineering. However, the change of scene did not work and he spent hours on the ocean shore contemplating the mysteries of life and searching for truth. He decided to abandon his studies and follow his calling. He went to Haridwar and though inspired by the Ganga, the hierarchal priesthood in the town did not impress him and he soon moved further, into the lap of the Himalayas.

With no worldly possessions and chanting the words "Narayan Narayan", he visited the four dhams — Gangotri, Yamunotri, Kedarnath and Badrinath. On the banks of the Bhilangana River near Tehri, he took sanyas and studied meditation techniques from a guru who named him 'NarayanNand'. He then moved to Uttarkashi and Gangotri where he studied scriptures and then spent five years in a cave in deep meditation. He was inspired to share his experiences with others and on the day of Dattatreya Jayanti went to Gangapur in Rajasthan. The gathering there was mesmerised by this tall good looking, soft-spoken young man with luminous eyes who could extensively quote from the scriptures and also sing bhajans in the most melodious, enchanting voice. Many believed Dattatreya himself had come down among them! This led to the formation of a small but dedicated group of disciples. He then travelled through Gujarat and on to Delhi before returning to the Himalayas to make his way to Kailash Mansarovar. He also spent several months at an ashram at Tapovan run by the sanyasin Ruma Devi.

Narayanswamy (as he was now known on account of his constantly chanting "Narayan! Narayan!!"), found this area on the route to Kailash particularly backward and extremely remote. He decided to set up an ashram to help the people of the area. In March 1936, the mahurat took place near Sosa village on what was then a barren hilltop, 9000 ft high. The villagers donated some land and some 'benami' land was acquired from the government. Using local materials and with limited funds from his followers, it took ten years to complete the ashram.

Narayanswamy was instrumental in spreading education in the area and many schools and an intermediate college were set up at Narayan Nagar near Askot and this proved a real boon for children who previously had to walk seven days to Almora to go to school. The ashram also set up basic medical facilities and undertook other development activities in the surrounding villages. In June 1954, Narayanswamy was diagnosed with cancer. After undergoing treatment in Calcutta, he returned to the hills but the deadly disease finally claimed him in November 1956. His dying wish was:

"See that the ashram, which has done its bit of service and brought awakening among people cut off from their more fortunate countrymen, is well cared for and not left in neglect. This is my only desire". The fact that the ashram is alive and running after fifty years of his demise shows that his followers have not let him down.

The inner sanctum at Narayanswamy Ashram

DAY 14
▸▸ Drive to Ranikhet

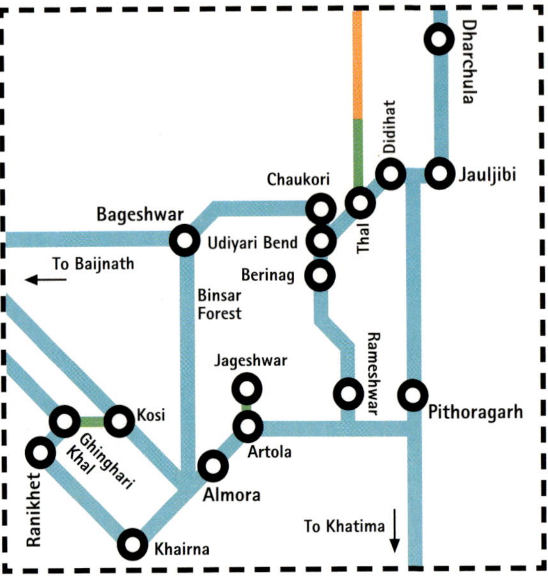

Dharchula-Pithoragarh	92 km		Rameshwar-Almora	76 km
Pithoragarh-Rameshwar	42 km		Almora-Ranikhet	45 km

Make sure that you tank up at Pithoragarh as fuel is not available till you hit Almora.

The next day involves a fair amount of driving as it is 255km to Ranikhet and takes around eight hours to get there. The route first takes you to Pithoragarh (5400ft/1646m), which is 92km, or three hours, from Dharchula. It is an extremely pretty drive along terraced fields and with a backdrop of snow capped mountains. The town, which is a district headquarter, is in a kind of natural bowl and does not have any views. The scenic drive continues on to Rameshwar, 42km further, which has a Shiva temple. Just ahead is the confluence of the Saryu and the Ram Ganga rivers and this is an ideal spot for a picnic lunch – the nearest dhaba is 27km further on. It is a

steady climb from the confluence till you reach
Artola, the place where you turn off to go to
Jageshwar. The route now takes you on to Almora
and then into Ranikhet ▪

**Storm brewing over
Ranikhet**

Pithoragarh-Lohaghat	67 km		Tanakpur-Khatima	24 km
Lohaghat-Champawat	13 km		Khatima-Rudrapur	73 km
Champawat-Tanakpur	75 km			

The Champawat area has a quiet charm of its own, and is not frequented by tourists. KMVN accommodation is probably your only option in this region.

The fifteenth and last day of travel, will take you to Corbett Park and on to Delhi. If you have another day to spend and have not yet lost your yen to see new places, you may like to stop and visit Lohaghat and Champawat, the ancient capital of the Katyuri kings.

Lohaghat, at 5740ft/1750m, is 67km from Pithoragarh. Just 6km short of town you turn off at Marodakhan and drive around 4km to Abbot Mount, which has panoramic views and at 6619ft/2018m is the highest point in this area. Lohaghat is set amongst tall deodar trees on the bank of the Loihawati River and was once the cultural capital of the Chand dynasty. The Kassite

Assyrians (who settled here after being evicted from Babylon by the Persians) are believed to have given this place its name.

Swami Vivekanand set up his Mayawati Ashram here in 1899. It is located 9km out of Lohaghat and is dedicated to "advaita and advaita alone". Also on the outskirts, 6km out, is the Kotalgarh Fort now in a state of ruins. According to legend, this was the stronghold of the demon Hanasur Daitya whose father, Mahabali, was involved in a prolonged battle with Vishnu. The blood spilt in this conflict accounts for the reddish colour of the soil, which in turn tinges the river a similar shade in the monsoon. From Lohaghat you can take a 47km rough drive to Pancheshwar at the confluence of the Saryu and Kali rivers. The Chaumu temple here is very popular with the locals and its annual festival attracts large crowds.

An interesting variation of the phrase 'buri nazar wale tera muh kala'!

Jacaranda trees are in
full bloom in May

Pancheshwar is also an angler's dream spot!
  Champawat is slightly lower at 5478ft/1670m and is only 13km from Lohaghat. The old structures of this former capital are in ruins but what remains of the Baleshwar and Ratneshwar temples is well worth a visit. These temples are from the fourteenth century and with their double shrines and 'mandapas' represent Kumaoni architecture at its best. The Hadimba temple, 3km away, is built on the mound where Vishnu assumed the Kurma or tortoise incarnation, and was called 'Kurmanchal' in the Skanda Purana.

It is a long haul to Delhi and unfortunately your descent to the plains is pretty rapid. In season a night spent at Corbett is a good way to break the journey.

You can take either of two routes back to Delhi. One way would be to drive to Almora (144km), and then onto Ranikhet and Corbett Park. The other route takes you down to Tanakpur, Khatima and onto Delhi via Rudrapur – a total distance of around 430km. This route is around 100km shorter than the first option, unless you choose to branch off at Rudrapur (towards Kashipur), to visit Corbett en route. If you do take this road, you can stop to see the pretty Shyamla Tal Lake. You have to turn off the main road 20km short of Tanakpur and drive 5km to get to the lake ■

FROM THE OTHER END OF THE SPECTRUM

DAY 1
▸▸ To Lansdowne via Meerut and Kotdwar (233km)

Delhi-Meerut	66 km	Kotdwar-Lansdowne	42 km
Meerut-Bijnor	65 km	Kotdwar-Pauri	111 km
Bijnor-Kotdwar	60 km		

Barring the section to Meerut, this route to Lansdowne is possibly the easiest and most pleasant of drives into the hills of Uttarakhand.

We recommend an early start as the 66km drive to Meerut can be a nightmare when traffic builds up. Also, to take the road leading to Bijnor and Kotdwar you have to drive through the city instead of just taking the bypass, and this is best negotiated in the early hours. Starting at the crack of dawn will save you a good 45 minutes or so.

Once you enter Meerut, drive across Begum Pul and take the road on the right, going to the army cantonment area and continue on to Mawana and Bijnor. This 65km can be covered in a little more than an hour as the road surface is good and traffic minimal. A good place to make a pit stop is 'Monty Millions' (!) restaurant located 26km before Bijnor, at the junction of the road leading to Muzaffarnagar.

From Bijnor to Najibabad is a short drive of 34km and another 26km gets you to Kotdwar, the town that serves as a gateway to the hills of this region. Lansdowne is a 42km drive from here and you have to turn off the main road to Pauri at Dugadda, 16km out of Kotdwar. This last section involves a reasonably steep ascent.

Lansdowne at 5600ft/1707m is a small quiet cantonment town, now the headquarters of the well-reputed army regiment, the Garhwal Rifles. The town is named after the 5th Marquis of Lansdowne (U.K.), Sir Henry Charles Keith Petty-Fitzmaurice, who was the British viceroy of India from 1888 to 1894.

The War Memorial at Lansdowne

St. John's Church, Lansdowne

Lansdowne is certainly not a destination for those looking for action – this is probably the quietest of our 'hill stations' and an ideal place to relax and unwind. It is a quaint small town of unspoilt beauty and time seems to perceptibly slow down here! There are charming walks over silver fir and pine laden slopes to view points predictably called – no marks for guessing – Tiffin Top and Snow View!

Garhwal Rifles has also created an artificial lake recently and boating is allowed here.

Graciously proportioned colonial bungalows are a steadfast reminder of the British Raj and there are two old churches you can visit. St. Mary's on the way to Tiffin Top is particularly interesting with its stained glass windows. The parade ground and adjoining war memorial are very impressive and impeccably maintained. The Darwan Singh

Museum has a fine armory on display and the
Garhwal Rifles' Mess is reputed to be one of the
finest in the country with its amazing array of
trophies and silver. The resident ghost, 'Major's
Ghost', is treated here with due deference —
traditionally banquet dinners start with a toast
raised to him under the grand crystal chandelier!

Accommodation is extremely limited with the
combined capacity of the GMVN Tourist Bungalow
and the sprawling and dignified Fairy Dale Hotel
being around fifteen rooms! The facilities are clean
but basic and there are no signs of any luxurious
infrastructure being developed. Even the main
market is a small but neat collection of shops and
dhabas around a square. The dhabas are renowned
for their delicious, incredibly large (bigger than a
dinner plate), paranthas ■

Magnificent Chaukhamba

DAY 2
▶▶ Drive to Pauri (84km)

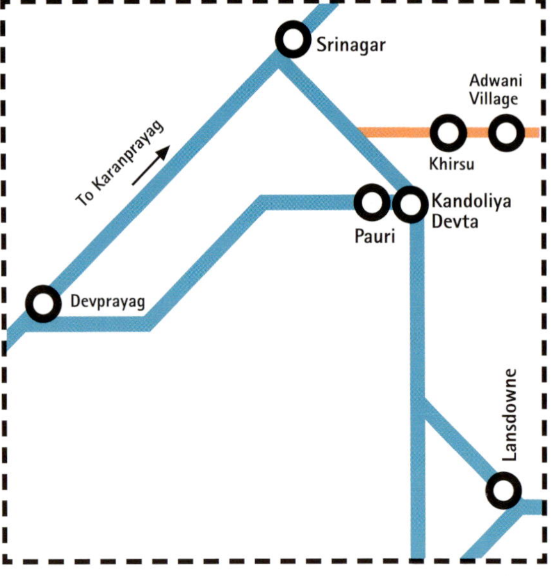

The forest above Pauri is a good place for great views as also for stretching your legs.

| Lansdowne-Gumkhal | 12 km | Pauri-Khirsu | 15 km |
| Gumkhal-Pauri | 73 km | Khirsu-Srinagar | 17 km |

Spend a relaxed morning soaking in the peaceful atmosphere or walking around this sleepy town and then drive out to Pauri after a late lunch. The drive takes around three hours and there is nothing to recommend Pauri other than its brilliant view of the Chaukhamba peak – and the fact that a stop here shortens the next day's journey to Dhanaulti via Devprayag.

You can stop by at the temple of Kandoliya Devta, located in a thick forest just 2km before Pauri. For the energetic, there is a steep 8km trek up to the eighth century Kyunkaleshwar Mahadev Temple dedicated to Shiva. This temple complex offers a lofty, panoramic view of the Chaukhamba, Neelkanth and Kedarnath peaks. If you happen to spend more time in Pauri, a day's excursion to Khirsu (15km) is very pleasant. There are plans to develop this pristine area into a resort and for all you know, in a few years this may be the place to visit!

The drive to Adwani village (17km), is also quite scenic and this is another place to explore out of Pauri.

There are some rather basic hotels in town but the only real choice you have is the GMVN Tourist Rest House which has a great location and is a good place to catch the snow views. In the busy season (May - October) it is advisable to book in advance as you would be really unhappy stuck in a crowded, uncomfortable place in town with no views to compensate.

The next day involves an early start not only for the views but also to let you get into Dhanaulti by late afternoon ■

No, it's not a notice to set down your camera — it actually does lead you to Lansdowne!

DAY 3
▸▸ Drive to Dhanaulti via Devprayag and Chamba (161km)

The view of the confluence at Devprayag is quite spectacular, but there is not much to commend the town and you can bypass it.

Pauri-Devprayag	45 km	Chamba-Dhanaulti	30 km
Devprayag-Rishikesh	68 km	Dhanaulti-Mussoorie	24 km
Devprayag-Chamba	86 km		

Your best chance of catching a good view of the snowy mountains is in the morning before 9 a.m. and we recommend you get up early enough to catch the softly lit peaks at dawn or the crystalline snows glistening in the morning sun, a little later.

A short 45km drive brings you to Devprayag where the Bhagirathi comes down and meets the Alaknanda. This is considered the second most important 'prayag' or confluence, after Prayagraj at Allahabad. Devprayag has two temples of some importance — the more famous being that of Raghunathji with its black granite image of

Vishnu. The smaller temple, known as the Bharat
Mandir, was used to house the idol of Bharatji
when Rishikesh was threatened by one of
Aurangzeb's religious purges. Devprayag is also
the home of the Badrinath 'pandas' or pandits. At
all times of the year, you will find devotees taking
a dip at the 'sangam', where the two rivers meet,
despite the freezing cold temperature of the water.

From here, it is a winding 86km (around three
hours) drive to Chamba, a rather non-descript
town. Your destination, Dhanaulti, is only 30km
further and this peaceful resort lies at a cool
7380ft/2250m altitude, making it the highest

**Heading home after a
day working the fields —
en route to Chamba**

developed hill resort in the region. With thick deodar forests and good views, it is a great place to spend the afternoon – or even a day or two. Although spill over from the bustling and overcrowded hill station of Mussoorie, only 24km away, does reach Dhanaulti during the peak tourist season, it is still not overrun by crowds. You can visit the nearby Surkhanda Devi Temple – this entails a steep 1.5km climb but affords great views on a clear day. The special religious significance of this temple is that it is located at the spot where Sati's head fell when Shiva was engaged in his great cosmic dance ■

An enticing glimpse of the Himalayas from Dhanaulti

⏩ Drive to Harsil via Chamba and Uttarkashi

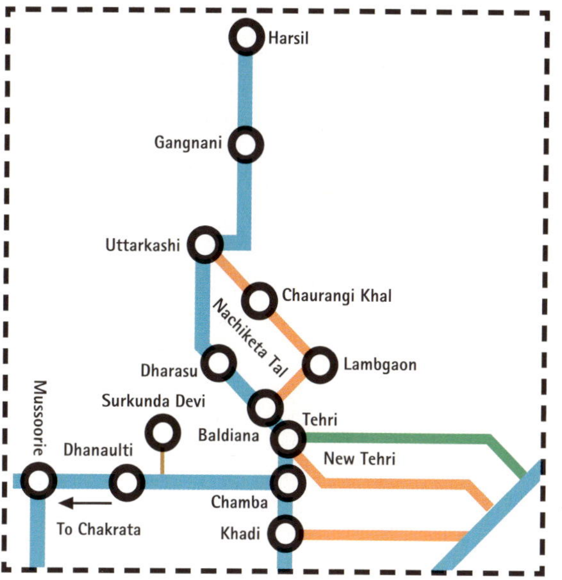

Beyond Chamba the standard of dhabas is not great – carry your lunch or settle for a late meal in Uttarkashi.

Dhanaulti – Chamba	30 km	Bhaldiana –	
Chamba – Bhaldiana	33 km	Chauranghi Khal	50 km
Bhaldiana – Uttarkashi	51 km	Chauranghi Khal –	
Uttarkashi – Gangnani	43 km	Uttarkashi	80 km
Gangnani – Harsil	31 km		

You have a long 188km drive ahead of you this day and an early start is called for as you will be on the road six to eight hours.

If you are in the mood to stretch your legs and explore a delightful, lesser-known lake – Nachiketa Tal, you will have to set out really bright and early as this diversion adds around three hours to your day's journey. It is a gradual 3km climb up through a beautiful thick forest before you come upon this lake, nestled and almost hidden among the trees at the crest of the hill.

En route to Harsil — these mountains are truly Shiva's abode; the hillsides are dotted with dedications to him

Your route to Harsil involves backtracking to Chamba and driving past the controversial Tehri Dam site to Bhaldiana, 33km from Chamba. Tehri was built as the capital of Garhwal in 1815 after Maharaj Sudarshan Sah was forced to cede half his kingdom, including the prevailing capital, to the British as pay-back for their assistance in driving out the invading Gorkha forces. Tehri remained the capital for over a hundred years, till 1924, when it was shifted to Narendra Nagar. Whatever remains from that period in this area is soon to be submerged and the inhabitants have been relocated to New Tehri that lies on a hill overlooking the dam. The palace at Narendra Nagar has been converted to an exclusive, and expensive, spa – the Ananda Spa and Resort.

Just ahead of Bhaldiana is the diversion that leads to Nachiketa Tal. At the milestone that reads 'Dharasu-22km', make a U-turn on to the road that heads down to Lambgaon. This detour to Uttarkashi is around 80km and adds 29km to the day's drive.

Though Nachiketa Tal is not a large lake, it is beautifully set, like a small gem in the dense forest surrounding it.

If you decide to follow this route, from Lambgaon you will have to take the road that climbs through dense forests to Chauranghi Khal, 30km short of Uttarkashi. You park the car at Chauranghi Khal and follow a well marked trail up to the lake that also has a temple on its shores. In March/April, the rhododendrons are in full bloom and if you enjoy a bit of climbing, this is a thoroughly enjoyable excursion.

To go directly to Harsil, you would continue to drive the balance 22km straight on to Dharasu and then 29km to Uttarkashi. (There is a turn-off for Yamunotri from Dharasu.)

Since you have to negotiate another 74km (approximately two to three hours driving time) to Harsil, you should aim to be in Uttarkashi by the

Nachiketa Tal

early afternoon so you can make it to your destination before sunset.

Leaving Uttarkashi, for the first 10km or so, you drive along a disappointingly thin stream of water that is more a nullah than the powerful Bhagirathi River you expect. This is the result of a 39m high barrage constructed at Maneri for the hydro-electric project there. This has reduced the river flow at Uttarkashi to a mere trickle during the winter and spring months when there is very little snow melt. Gangnani, 43km down the road, has hot springs where you can stop for a relaxing, well-deserved dip if your time schedule permits.

The high point, Sukhi (9020ft/2750m), is 18km further and beyond it you descend 300m to the bridge at Jhala. Harsil is barely 6km away and is a place of compelling beauty and natural grandeur. The stately mountains seem to be at touching distance here and the Bhagirathi, with its startling clear blue waters, gushes through a broad river bed hemmed by tall deodar trees.

  The only accommodation available is at the GMVN Tourist Bungalow that enjoys a brilliant location and is reasonably comfortable. If you happen to be at Harsil just before or after the peak season, this is actually a great place to spend a

Mountain peaks practically envelope you at Harsil

The Bhagirathi River at Harsil

couple of days just soaking in Nature's beauty. The food at the Tourist Bungalow is good but basic and you might want to carry some additional food items to supplement the fare available. (In case you are wondering about not seeing Uttarkashi, this is best done on the return journey when you will have more time at hand) ■

DAY 5
▶▶ Drive to Gangotri and return to Harsil

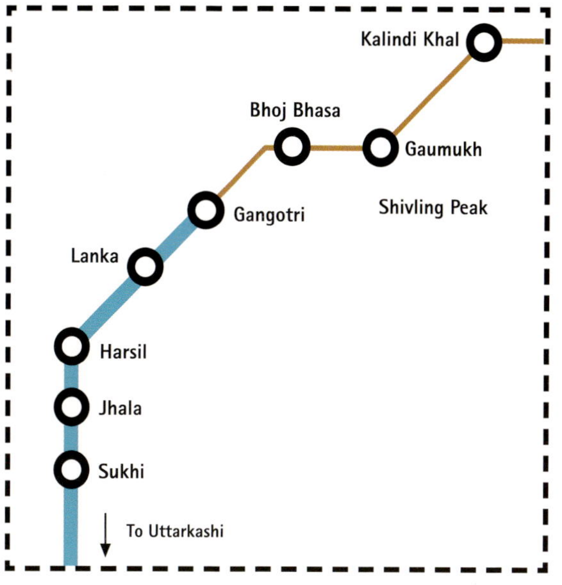

Gangotri gets very crowded during the pilgrim season and at that time is not the best place to spend a night. If you do plan to, book accommodation in advance.

| Harsil – Lanka | 11 km | Gangotri – Gaumukh | 17 km |
| Lanka – Gangotri | 11 km | Gaumukh – Tapovan | 4 km |

It is only a 44km return journey to Gangotri and one can be back at Harsil to enjoy the sylvan surroundings by lunch. The drive up is through spectacular forest and mountain scenery with the Sudarshan Peak at 20,175ft/6151m, looming like a sentinel over the valley as one gets closer. Around 14km short of Gangotri you cross a suspension bridge that is 123m above the rushing river. Crossing this is a thrill and it is supposed to be one of the highest bridges.

There is an interesting legend that tells of the ghost of an Englishman riding his gray horse along a rocky trail on full moon nights. The antecedents of F.E. Wilson are unclear but he settled here and married a local girl, called Sangrami and built a

grand bungalow – Wilson Hut, on the road to Gangotri. He grew in power and influence and was referred to as Raja Wilson. In the 1860's when a suspension bridge was built over the Jadh Ganga at Bhairon Ghati, the locals were too scared to use it till Pahari Wilson leapt onto his stallion and galloped up and down the bridge to allay their fears. Now, years later, the river is believed to weep in sympathy to the restless hoof beats of his ghost riding through!

The temple, 9892ft/3016m, is a modest structure with a small silver image of goddess Ganga. Adjacent to the temple is the stone where King

While staying at Harsil, do take the time to walk the beautiful environs enveloping it – the people here are extremely helpful and will point you in the right direction.

Bhagirath performed his penance to induce the goddess to descend to earth.

The actual source of the river Bhagirathi, or Ganga, lies at Gaumukh and getting there entails a two-day trek of 17km each way. You could spend the first night 14km from Gangotri at Bhoj Bhasa (12,350ft/3800m), which has a spectacular view of the Shivling peak. However, some believe Gaumukh is not the main source since less than 1km beyond the snout, the stream is visible at Nandanvan. According to this theory, the main source of the Ganga is either the Gangotri peak or the Narayan Parbat, the source of the Alaknanda ■

Don't miss the beautiful nose rings

THE DIVINE DESCENT OF GODDESS GANGA

The chain of events which led to the divine descent of the Ganga lie in the realms of Hindu mythology. In ancient times, King Sagar was successful in slaying the demons that were troubling the earth. In order to commemorate this victory, he embarked on the 'Ashwamedh Yagya' — an elaborate religious ceremony to proclaim his supremacy. This yagya entailed sending a symbolic royal white horse, followed by his troops, to the far flung areas of

the kingdom — if unchallenged, his supremacy would be confirmed. However, this move did not find favour with Indra and apprehensive of losing out in the power hierarchy, he stole the horse and tethered it close to the ashram where the great sage Kapila was in meditative retreat. The king's 60,000 sons succeeded in tracing the missing stallion but in the process disturbed the meditating sage. Enraged, he opened his eyes and all those who came into his sight were instantly turned to ashes. The only survivor of this mass immolation was their half brother Asamanjas, who returned to tell the tale. The king's grandson, Anshuman retrieved the horse and was advised by Kapila that the only way the king's sons could enter heaven was if the Ganga came and cleansed their ashes with her holy water. Anshuman went into deep meditation to seek the blessings of the gods for this Herculean task. He was unsuccessful and it was his grandson, King Bhagirath whose 'tapasya' finally persuaded the gods to intervene. However, the goddess Ganga was just not interested in leaving her abode in the heavens and only with the collective persuasive powers of the other gods did she reluctantly agree to descend to earth. Still annoyed, she came down with enough force to wash away the earth. It was left to Shiva to save the situation and he received the torrent in the locks of his matted hair dividing it into seven streams. These are the Bhagirathi, Janhvi, Rishiganga, Saraswati, Alaknanda, Bhilangana and Mandakini, which merge with each other at various points, culminating in a final confluence at Devprayag to flow thereon as the Ganga.

DAY 6

▸▸ Drive to Uttarkashi, Dharasu Bend and Barkot (160km)

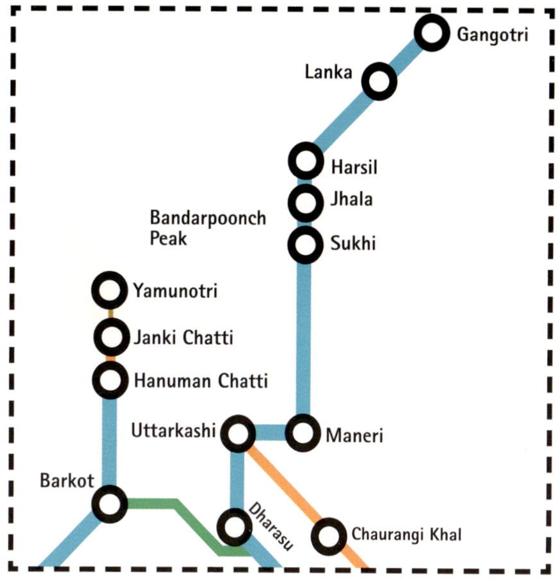

Uttarkashi is a popular destination for pilgrims. During season, be prepared for crowds at the main temples but do not let this deter you from those of your choice.

Harsil - Uttarkashi	74 km	Barkot - Hanuman Chatti	42 km
Uttarkashi - Dharasu	28 km	Hanuman Chatti -	
Dharasu - Barkot	58 km	Yamunotri	13 km

You can take it easy this morning and time your departure so you get to Uttarkashi in time for a relaxed lunch and a bit of sightseeing. The onward journey to Barkot (86km), should not take more than three hours. Since Barkot is merely a staging point (albeit an extremely scenic one), for the next day's drive, you can even leave Uttarkashi as late as 3 p.m.

Loosely translated, Uttarkashi means 'Kashi (Varanasi) of the North' and, as always, there is a legend explaining this. According to a story in the Puranas, Shiva visualised the possibility of Kashi

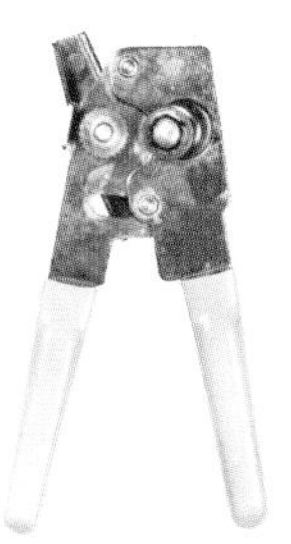

being plagued by religious persecution and foretold the establishment of a similar township in a remote place. Like Varanasi, Uttarkashi is situated between two streams – the Varuna and Assi and the ghats bear the same names. At some time in the distant past, a replica of the lingam in Kashi appeared in the temple dedicated to Lord Vishwanath, the most important temple here. Within its courtyard lies the Shakti Temple that holds a massive 26ft high brass trident with a base circumference of almost 9ft!

This town is the stage for a large fair and festival spread over seven days on 'Makarsakranti', which falls in mid-January. Despite the freezing cold thousands of devotees take a dip in the frigid waters of the holy river. Gods and goddesses from all the neighbouring villages are brought down on their palanquins, women are bedecked in vibrant clothes and chunky jewellery, colourful shops spring up and there is much gaiety and festivity in the town.

An even bigger celebration is that of Shiva's birthday in July/August, which is marked with great fanfare.

Uttarkashi has several other interesting temples worth visiting and the more popular ones are the temples of Parshuram, Kali, Ekadash, Rudra and that of Sri Chandreshwara which overlooks the town. Two kilometers before entering the town, you can climb up to the temple of Kuteki Devi who is worshipped as a form of Durga. The temple was built by a daughter of the Maharaja of Kota, at a spot indicated to her by the Devi who appeared in a dream. Amazingly, both the Kuteki Devi and main Vishwanath temples escaped unscathed during the devastating earthquake in 1991 that claimed several lives and caused extensive damage to buildings.

Inhaling deeply! Sadhus and pilgrims flock to Uttarkashi

India's premiere mountaineering institute, named after our first prime minister, Jawaharlal Nehru, is located here. Besides many other distinguished climbers, the first Indian woman to climb Mt. Everest, Bachendri Pal, was trained here.

It is not easy to find accommodation in this town during the pilgrim season (May-October), and you should make your bookings in advance. After concluding your sightseeing, drive on to Barkot, which lies on the road to Yamunotri (the road ends 50km ahead of Barkot) ■

YAMUNOTRI

The temple of Yamunotri lies at an altitude of 10,447ft/3185m, at the foot of Kalind Parbat (14,501ft/4421m), the source of the Yamuna River. It stands on the western flank of the perennially snow clad Banderpoonch peak (20,713ft/6315m), against a backdrop of a magnificent waterfall that drops dramatically at this point. Nearby are hot springs where steaming water spurts into 'kunds' — the most important being the Surya Kund and pilgrims dip rice or potatoes loosely tied in cloth into these waters and when cooked, literally in minutes, this is treated as 'prasad'.

To reach it, you drive 107km from Yamuna Pul to Hanuman Chatti where the road ends. It is a 13km trek from the road head and this valley is rich in medicinal herbs and fruit trees. There is a GMVN Tourist Bungalow at Janki Chatti, 5km before Yamunotri.

The temple is not a very impressive structure and holds a small image of the goddess Yamuna who is the daughter of Surya, the sun god, and twin sister of Yama, the god of death. Bathing in its waters is supposed to spare devotees from a painful death. The temple is literally a shelter over the spring revered as the source of the Yamuna. Nearby is the Dibya Shila, which is worshipped before puja is offered at the main temple.

While returning one can also visit the Someshwar Temple at Kharsali across the river at Janki Chatti. The 'pandas' of Yamunotri belong to Kharsali village.

DAY 7

▶▶ Visit Hanol (81km), Tons Valley, Netwar, Lakhamandal en route to Mussoorie (271km)

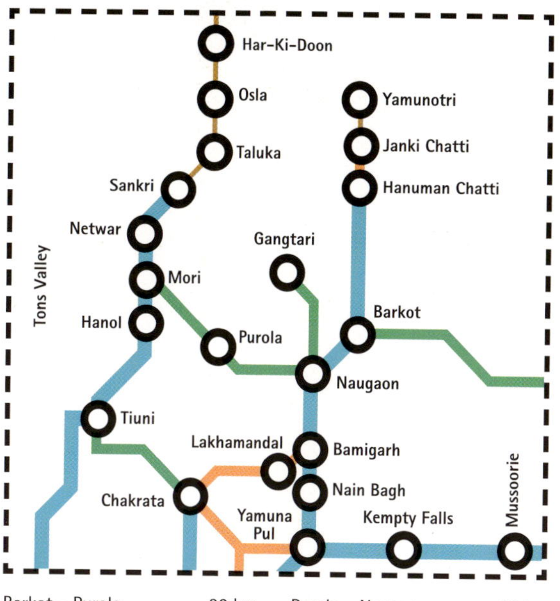

There are no petrol pumps in the area, so ensure that you start with a full tank from Uttarkashi.

Barkot – Purola	28 km	Purola – Naugaon	19 km
Purola – Mori	37 km	Naugaon – Lakhamandal	18 km
Mori – Hanol	16 km	Lakhamandal – Nain Bagh	37 km
Mori – Netwar	11 km	Nain Bagh – Mussoorie	41 km

Hopefully, spending minimal time on the road the past few days have allowed you to recharge your batteries as this day entails a long haul of 271km (9-10 hours of driving).

You drive through wonderfully scenic countryside as you traverse the great river valleys of the Yamuna and its tributary, the Tons. An extremely viable option is to spend another night at Barkot, a day trip to Hanol & Netwar and drive to Mussoorie, via Lakhamandal, the next day.

If you are travelling in the months of May and June it would make an exhilarating break to

The Tons is a delightful, frisky river and a great place to go rafting — or just spend time by. It is the most important tributary of the Yamuna.

spend a couple of days en route at the Himalayan River Runners rafting camp between Mori and Hanol, in the Tons Valley. The river may look calm but there are some exciting rapids here that are guaranteed to bring on that adrenalin rush!

The first leg of the drive takes you via Naugaon to Purola — a distance of 28km. Mori lies 37km further, on the banks of the rushing Tons River that, according to legend, was born of the tears of

**Prayers before a
sacrifice is made to
Mahasu Devta at Hanol**

the demoness Srupanakha. This river has great
stretches for rafting and kayaking and there is
plenty of trout in it for anglers but you will have
to obtain a permit from the DFO at Purola. The
drive from Tiuni to Mori is a sheer visual delight
with the road winding alongside the meandering
river and terraced fields catching slanting rays of
the sun.

From Mori it is only a 16km drive to the ancient

A Jaunsari Temple

temple complex at Hanol, which sits on a bluff above the river. This temple is dedicated to the reigning local deity, Mahasu Devta, who is worshipped devoutly throughout the Jaunsar Bawar area and Tons Valley. The main temple is a pagoda-like structure with a burnished copper roof and three spires glinting in the sunlight against the backdrop of a cerulean sky. The inner chamber holds statues of the deities clad in ornate clothing and women are only allowed up to the outer chamber. By the side of the temple are some small stone temples and ancient rock slabs of religious and mythical significance. There are two large spherical rocks, each with a diameter of one foot, and it is believed that only the pure-hearted can lift these!

Mahasu Devta holds a position of great reverence and esteem and there are two versions, or myths, regarding his presence here: Just before Hanol is a prosperous looking village called Maindrath and ages ago a Brahmin named Bhatt lived here with his family. A demon, Kirmir, made his appearance downstream and began to attack and feast on these villagers everyday. According to one version, in answer to his prayers, the Brahmin had a dream instructing him to go to Kashmir and locate four Mahasu brothers living there and appeal for their help. He did so and with their divine intervention, the demon was slain and the eldest revered henceforth as Mahasu Devta.

In the other version Bhatt, the Brahmin, prayed to his mentor, Shiva, for help and was directed to another devotee in the adjoining village. This devotee, a lady, had four sons and under Shiva's guidance directed Bhatt to plough the field at Hanol. While doing so, he came upon four 'shivlings' in the field and they took the form of the sons, Mahasu, Pavasi, Vasik and Chalda who,

Pick a spot between Mori and Hanol for a picnic lunch — on the waters edge if you choose.

with the help of Shiva's divine powers, overcame the demon. Mahasu Devta is therefore regarded as a representation of Shiva and a guardian deity. With its beautiful location, striking temples and captivating stories, Hanol definitely warrants a stop.

After this, you return to Mori and drive 11km up the valley to the village of Netwar that lies at the confluence of the Rupin and Supin rivers. From here these two rivers flow as the Tamasa or Tons, which meets the Yamuna further at Kalsi. There is a small wooden pagoda-shaped temple here that is dedicated to a local deity called Pokhu who is believed to be attendant to Shiva and deputy of Karna (the first-born – and abandoned – Pandava who fought on behalf of the Kauravas in the epic battle of *Mahabharata*). Pokhu is supposed to mete terrible and unrelenting punishment on wrong-doers and as a result, petty crime and theft are practically unknown here. Since it is believed that his face would horrify anyone, no devotees are allowed to see it and even the priest stands with his back to the idol when worshipping him!

The approach to this temple is through a thick forest rich in sounds and colours but the road that leads across the river is extremely rough and was non-existent in parts due to land slips when we negotiated it. This 6km round trip could take you more than an hour and is best avoided if you are driving on to Mussoorie and not spending time by the river.

However, if you are going to be in the area for a couple of days, there are some fascinating temples here, steeped in a unique and rich mythical tradition.

There is a beautiful old wooden temple, set in a courtyard, that is dedicated to Karna. This is in the village of Sarnaul, approximately a 2km climb up

This valley is steeped in the *Mahabharata* tradition — its legends have been woven inextricably in the fabric of life here. Even the 'villain of the piece', Duryodhan, and his clan the Kauravas, command a following!

A typical, brightly painted village home in the Jaunsari region

from Netwar. Temples to Karna are rare and there is another one in the region at the village of Deora. An interesting festival held at the Deora Temple is the 'festival of ball' during Makarsakranti — a competitive ball game is played between the 'Kaurava' and 'Pandava' teams and the ball is called 'Ghatotkach'. (Since this is a Kaurava-dominated area, this is a derogatory reference to the Pandava strongman, Bhim's son who was killed in battle).

The entire Tons valley, the Har-ki-Doon area and in fact Jaunsar Bawar (the triangular region between the Yamuna and the Tons rivers), is rich in the tradition of the *Mahabharata*. It is fascinating to learn that the villages along this route claim descent from either the Pandavas or the Kauravas. Particularly interesting is the fact that in the entire Netwar, Har-ki-Doon belt,

One of the many sculptures excavated around the Lakhamandal Temple complex

Kauravas are not only held in great esteem but Duryodhan, considered the 'villain of the piece' by most, is worshipped like any other deity – in fact, he rules supreme in these parts!

This is an area of hypnotising beauty and apparently the people here live in harmony with their natural environs and consider happiness, rather than money and material goods, of paramount importance. Legend has it, during Dwapar Yuga, King Duryodhan travelled through beautiful lands but when he came to Hanol, he was mesmerised by its sheer beauty and appealed to Mahasu Devta to grant this land to him. He was given it on the condition he would always look after its people. This entire region of sporadic villages is the domain of Duryodhan Maharaj and his spirit is said to enter mediums called 'Mali', to give orders, judgements and guidance. These 'orders' are taken as final and indisputable, so much so that these villages seldom approach Patwaris and other officials!

There are temples dedicated to Duryodhan Maharaj in these villages but the most important and main temple is at Jakhol and this is the only one with an idol of the deity. This idol is taken out during certain times and carried to the other village temples by turn. The Duryodhan Temple at Osla is approachable only by foot — 12km beyond Netwar, is the village of Sankri and from here Osla is a 26km trek along the much-favoured Har-ki-Doon trail.

After lunch on the banks of the river, retrace your path to Purola and Naugaon. From there you drive 12km down the valley towards Bamigad and a kilometer before town, cross the bridge over the river to Chakrata (67km), and Lakhamandal (6km).

Lakhamandal is a 'yet-to-be-discovered' gem — a small, serene village with a lovely temple complex. The main temple has some stone idols that are a fine example of the exquisite workmanship prevalent many centuries ago — some of them date back to the fifth century. There

Assuming you have limited time but want to check out another temple, take a 1.5km walk above Netwar to the Karna Temple.

After leaving Lakhamandal don't worry if your fuel gauge is on the low side — there is a petrol pump at Nain Bagh, around 25km away.

are two life size statues of the 'dwarpals', Jai and Vijay, and two impressive, large stone 'shivlings'. The complex is under the control of the ASI (Archaeological Survey of India), and according to locals, the locked godown holds many more priceless treasures unearthed here. There is also an ancient cave near the village. This spot is believed to be the place where Duryodhan conspired to burn the Pandavas alive in the 'Lakshyagriha', a house especially constructed with shellac. True or

The main temple at Lakhamandal

not, judging by the number and intricate work on the statues found here, this was certainly a place of religious significance.

To get to Mussoorie, you cross back to the main road and drive 31km to Nain Bagh (where petrol is available), and a further 12km to Yamuna Pul. Your destination is a 29km ascending drive from here, via Kempty Falls. The road surface is good, traffic negligible and one can make good time on this 72km section (allow two to three hours) ■

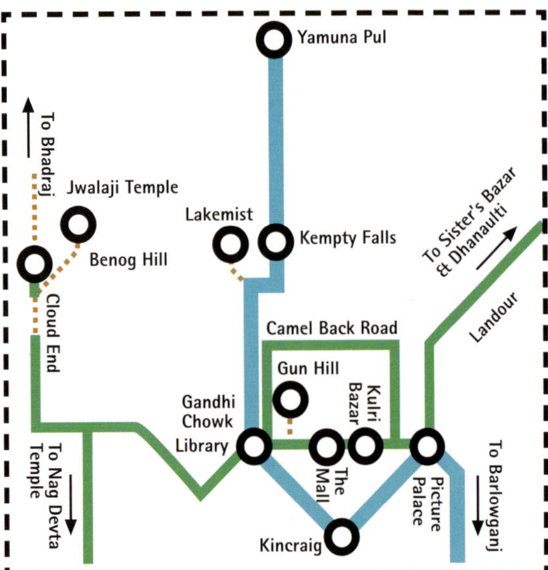

DAYS 8 & 9
▸▸ Mussoorie (6560ft/2000m)

During season tourists throng to Mussoorie and the roads are choked with traffic. Visit it off-season to really enjoy this 'Queen of the Hills'.

Mussoorie, the erstwhile 'Queen of the Hills' has certainly lost some of its dignity and grandeur and gets completely overrun by tourist traffic during the peak season (May-June). At this time, Mussoorie closely resembles Churchgate railway station in Mumbai, during rush hour! It can be a veritable nightmare with crowds thronging the Mall and ugly traffic snarls trapping you even 3km before you enter the town!!

However, this is only one face of Mussoorie – the ugly one; make a visit here just before, or after the peak tourist season and you will see the gracious beauty that this hill station was famous for. The air is pure, the climate invigorating and the interesting architecture, majestic mountains and beautiful walks through stately deodars can

A princely summer
home at Mussoorie

Not a 'negli–gible' array of negligee's for a hill station — catering to honeymooners who throng to Mussoorie!

all actually be enjoyed when you aren't being jostled by crowds and assaulted by noise!

Mussoorie was originally 'discovered' by Capt. Young in the 1820s, and till he built his house below Landour, this was a spot used only for grazing by local cowherds. Initially developed as a military convalescent center, by mid-nineteenth century it became a popular resort for the British to escape the summer heat. A few years later, Indian royalty started building summer residences here. Today Mussoorie's main claim to fame is the Lal Bahadur Shastri Academy where the steel frame of India — its bureaucrats, receive their initial dose of how to successfully manage (mismanage?) things!

One of the most popular excursions is the 2km walk, or 400m cable car ride, to the summit of

Gun Hill (7000ft/2134m). This is the best place for breathtaking views of Banderpoonch (20,713ft/6315m), Kedarnath (22,304ft/6800m), Badrinath (22,478ft/6853m) and even Nanda Devi (25,640ft/7817m) in the far distance. Gun Hill gets its name from the peculiar custom of firing a cannon at noon every day during the British Raj. The official reason was to provide the locals with the correct time but quite possibly, it was designed to get them cracking after the morning chai break!

There are some other good walks – one being the 3km loop on the Camel's Back road, above Kulri Bazaar, which has good mountain views. A longer 5km walk takes you to Landour Bazaar and up to Lal Tiba, which at 8000ft/2439m, is the highest point in town. You could also stroll down to Happy Valley and the Tibetan Refugee Center where you can admire their handicrafts and maybe sample the local 'chaang' (rice wine).

For those seeking a more peaceful commune with Nature, there are some good off-track walks through forested patches in the Landour and Cloud's End area.

The Mall is, of course, where the action is, with numerous restaurants, dhabas, and well-stocked shops. Judging by the amazing array of neglige's hung outside shops, the offers of 'honeymoon packages' and even its very own Honeymoon Inn (a la Holiday Inn!), this is obviously quite the sought after destination for starry eyed 'just marrieds'!!

Approximately 6km from Mussoorie, on Cart Road, is the ancient temple of Nag Devta. The Jwalaji Temple, dedicated to Durga, is atop the richly forested Benog Hill that once held an Observatory.

One of the most popular attractions around here is Kempty Falls, around 15km along the

You certainly will not be short of places to eat in Mussoorie but the Awadhi cuisine at Carlton Hotel is particularly good, as is the multi-cuisine at Tavern Restaurant.

Gluttony??
We haven't checked this
one out!!

Mussoorie-Chakrata road. These falls were 'discovered' and developed by John Mekinen and became a preferred spot for evening tea parties. The name probably owes its origin to these parties which were referred to as 'camp-tea'! The falls themselves are quite spectacular, particularly during, and just after, the rains. The cascade splits into five falls and the largest is 40ft high. You can walk down to the bottom of the falls where water collects in a pool that many enjoy taking a dip in.

Unfortunately Kempty is no longer the idyllic place this description might lead you to believe! There is a rash of cheek-by-jowl shops and eateries at the road head, litter is strewn everywhere and parking is difficult to find. Matters seem to worsen every year with dhabas

now creeping all the way down to the pond at the
bottom. It really saddens the heart to see how the
blinkered, lop-sided policies of the administration
and short-sightedness of businessmen have raped
the countryside.

In case you do go to see the falls, you would be
better off avoiding the crowded eateries here and
rather stop for a quiet coffee and sandwich at
Lake Mist Resort, located around 3km from here.

If you plan to visit Mussoorie, we would
certainly recommend going there at any time
other than the peak summer, or Dussehra/Puja
break. A stay, off-season, in one of the delightful
'old-world' hotels like the Carlton, Padmini Niwas,
Savoy or Kasmanda Palace will give you a
glimpse of Mussoorie in its hey day ■

**The Mall at a rare
peaceful moment of
time....**

DAYS 10
▸▸ To Chakrata via Dehradun

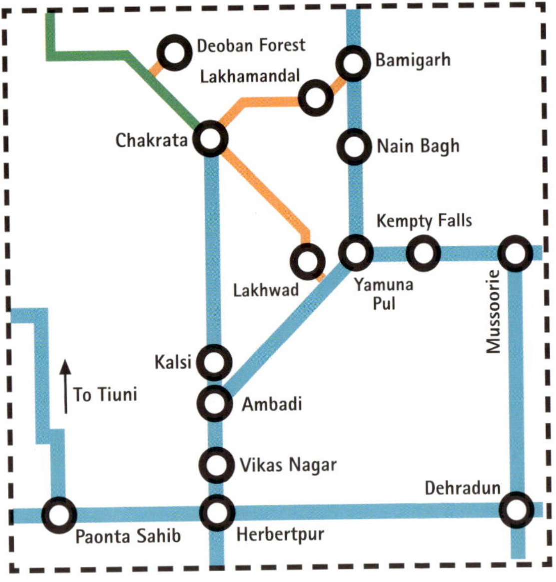

There is an alternate route via Yamuna Pul to Chakrata. Though almost 50km shorter, there is no significant time saving due to the nature of the terrain.

Mussoorie – Chakrata via Yamuna Pul	78 km	
Mussoorie – Dehradun	35 km	
Dehradun – Herbertpur	36 km	
Herbertpur – Kalsi		14 km
Kalsi – Chakrata		42 km
Herbertpur – Paonta Sahib		13 km

It is a 35km (one hour) drive down to Dehradun, the capital of Uttarakhand. Located at 2300ft/701m, the city is also well known for the erstwhile institutions, Indian Military Academy (IMA) and Doon School, which are based here. However, this once sylvan valley has grown exponentially and is now a completely built, large township.

Dehradun, nestled between the Himalayas and the Shivalik hills, has seen many a political upheaval through its history — occupied by the Muslim Governor of Saharanpur in the late eighteenth century, many invaders subsequently swept through it, the Gorkhas from Nepal being

Dehradun's landmark –
the Ghanta Ghar

the last rulers before the British took over in 1815.

Although we do not recommend staying here, there are a few places worth a 'dekho'.

'Dehra' means camp and the town acquired its name after Ram Rai, the son of the 7th Sikh Guru, Har Rai, established a base here after he was denied succession. The gurudwara established in the seventeenth century at Jhanda Mohalla is still a popular destination for Sikh devotees.

The imposing Forest Research Institute, one of the finest institutes of forest sciences in the world and the Indian Military Academy are definitely worth a visit.

The Tapkeshwar Mahadev Cave Temple, dedicated to Shiva, is located at Bhori village. The name

The grand Forest Research Institute (FRI) building – now called the Indira Gandhi National Forest Academy

comes from the continuous dripping of water on the sacred 'lingam' from the roof of the cave.

The headquarters of the Survey of India is located here and in the past, this place saw hectic, path-breaking work by geographers and trained locals (called 'pundits'). They undertook many an undercover trip to map territories not only in India but beyond its borders, in Afghanistan and Tibet. It took them years of travel at great risk and with the aid of very elementary tools, to map and establish that the Tsang Po River in China and the Brahmaputra were the same! This is where, after extensive calculation, Peak XV, at 29028ft/8848m, was determined to be the highest mountain in the world. Supposedly, considerable time was spent in

Stop at Kwality's on the road leading into town from Mussoorie.... famous for its toffees, fondly called 'Kwal-Toffs'.

trying to ascertain the peak's local name (for centuries known as the Chomolangma in Tibet and Sagarmatha in Nepal), but according to reports, they drew a blank and so decided to name it after George Everest, the former Surveyor General! The reason for breaking the convention of using local names is a mystery but the case made by many for renaming the peak is certainly strong.

From Dehradun, you drive past the IMA to Herbertpur (36km), where you turn right towards Vikas Nagar and Kalsi. If you have the time, and inclination, you can make a 13km detour from here to the scenic Sikh gurudwara at Paonta Sahib.

Chakrata (7003ft/2135m) is only 56km from Herbertpur, but the hill section drive is limited to a 30kmph speed. The road beyond Kalsi is under military control and foreigners need a special permit from the Home Ministry to proceed.

Paonta Sahib Gurudwara   Traffic movement is one-way and the gate opens

every 2.5 hours from 7 a.m. in the summer. Kalsi has a second century BC Ashoka rock edict but you have to walk down a short path towards the river bank to see it.

Chakrata is a high security military cantonment, established 125 years ago by Col. Hume of the 55th Regiment. It is here that the Special Forces undergo rigorous training with covert operations being rehearsed in this isolated place.

The drive is not very interesting but just as you approach Chakrata, you pass through a beautiful deodar forest. The town enjoys a magnificent view of the greater Himalayas with the Banderpoonch massif dominating the skyline. It is a quiet, charming little place spread over a ridge cloaked in a rich green cover of deodars, oaks and rhododendrons. Chakrata is not at all built-up and the houses you see either follow the quaint local architectural style or are pretty colonial buildings. The accommodation available here is rather basic and Chakrata has little else to offer besides its serene environ and sylvan charm. The dense, virgin forests are dotted with attractive Jaunsari villages. From here you can access Mundali (9000ft/2744m) where skiing is possible in the winter months, Deoban Forest Reserve (9397ft/2865m), Kanasar Forest (8500ft/2592m) and Kathiyan (7000ft/2134m).

The day you arrive, you can make a short trip to Tiger Falls, only 5km along the Mussoorie road. This water fall is one of the highest in the country and is a walk of just over 1km from the road.

There are a couple of excellent day trips that can be made out of here and we recommend one – or both – for the next day. If you choose to do only one of these excursions and would prefer a more comfortable night's stay, you can drive back to Mussoorie, via Lakhamandal on this day ■

Chakrata is primarily a military base and its remote location is an ideal training ground for covert operations..... watch out for spy vs spy action!

DAY 11

▶▶ Around Chakrata and drive to Rishikesh or Mussoorie

The region receives heavy snowfall. Deoban and Kanasar can be cut off as late into the season as the first week of April.

Chakrata – Deoban	16 km	Chakrata – Dehradun	92 km
Deoban – Kanasar	30 km	Dehradun – Rishikesh	46 km
Chakrata – Kanasar	28 km	Rishikesh - Narendra Nagar	17 km

Deoban (9397ft/2365m) is 16km from Chakrata and is one of the most pristine forests you would have encountered. The drive, however, is very rough and you may even want to hire a vehicle for this excursion rather than challenge your car's suspension! You initially climb through a rocky stretch with the road clinging to the edge of rather precipitous drops. You then drive through a thick forest of tall deodars and as you crest the hill, the trees dramatically give way to an undulating rich-green alpine meadow — idyllic with dappled sunlight. There is a hundred-year old colonial

Forest Rest House here and a stream running close
by, making it an ideal place for Nature lovers to
camp. Day trippers should bring a packed lunch;
walk through the quiet of this verdant forest to the
very top where you can get sensational views of
the big mountains. Especially recommended is a
post-lunch lie-back on the rolling green carpet
with the smell of fresh grass, the hypnotising
sound of cicadas and the stunning blue skies
above....

Kanasar is 28km away, on a tightly winding road
with a rough surface but the forests and stunning
scenery (particularly at sunset) make this drive a
most memorable one. According to the proudly
displayed signage of the Forest Department, this
forest is rated as the best deodar forest in Asia
and has a towering deodar, believed to have the
largest girth of any in Asia! As the road dips in to

Dusk at Kanasar

THE JAUNSARIS

The area around Chakrata is part of a region called Jaunsar Bawar and the Jaunsari tribals here have a fascinating culture. They were comparatively undisturbed even during the British rule as this was designated a scheduled area and even today there is controlled access to parts of the region due to army presence. This isolation allowed them to cling to their customs and beliefs though mainstream influences are now changing many of them.

The Jaunsaris believe they are descendants of the Pandavas. Mahasu Devta commands tremendous reverence and his blessing, or ire, is of utmost consequence. As a people they are colourful, joyous and friendly and rather different from the other major tribal group of the area — the Bawars, who claim to descend from the Kauravas, live in remote places at higher altitudes and tend to be more taciturn. The two tribes prefer not to intermarry.

As most tribals, the Jaunsaris lived in perfect harmony with their environment and their belief system stands testimony to this. They are guided by 'Matris' or 'Paris' (fairies) and 'Suchcha Matri' presides over the forest and wildlife while 'Masaan Matri' controls lower levels like streams, rivers and cremation grounds. These Matris communicate to them through mediums called 'Malis'. The Jaunsaris protect the Matris' domain and reportedly will not even shout in the forest — they seek permission for any felling or killing that is deemed necessary for their existence. A brilliant tradition of environment protection!!

They have colourful festivals and even their homes are painted in vibrant shades to reflect their personalities. They practiced both polyandry and polygamy but this is changing with each generation. The birth of a girl child is very welcome and they do not have a dowry system. In fact, the boy and his family pay a bride-price which is returned in case of a divorce, once the girl comes back.

Jaunsaris still prefer to barter and the village elders are consulted for all communal affairs and disputes. Following a quaint tradition, a 'shehnai' player and drummer play to announce dusk and dawn to the entire village!

The Jaunsari temples are also quite unique in their character, being elaborately decorated with animal horns and masks on the exterior. The inner sanctum is however more in conformity with Hindu temples and the deity is adorned with elaborate trappings.

The door to the temple
at Netwar

a valley, you come upon a delightful meadow with sun filtering through tall trees, the tinkling of grazing cattle and a tiny, colourful mandir – a scene of picture postcard beauty and a perfect place to take a break.

From Chakrata, you can either drive to Dehradun and on to Rishikesh or proceed to Mussoorie. Lakhamandal is 60km along the road to Mussoorie and the entire drive will take four to five hours, bringing you there in time for dinner.

If you are taking the Dehradun route, make sure you catch either the 1430 or 1700 hours slot at the traffic gate to Kalsi so you can reach your destination before it gets late. Rishikesh is only 46km from Dehradun and the journey will take an hour. The choice between spending another night at Mussoorie's lofty heights or enjoying the river at Rishikesh is entirely yours to make ■

A sun dappled meadow and the Kanasar Devi Temple near the Forest Rest House

DAY 12

▸▸ Rishikesh

If you have spent the night at Mussoorie, you will have to factor in a two hour drive down to Rishikesh.

From time immemorial Rishikesh (which literally interprets as 'hair of the sages'), has been a holy pilgrim spot. It was the camp for devotees and sages alike to come together to pay homage to Mother Ganga before ascending to other pilgrim centers in the lofty Himalayan peaks.

Situated on the right bank of the Ganga and regarded as the celestial abode of gods, it is believed that Bharat, Rama's brother, underwent severe penance here. Later a temple dedicated to him was constructed at this site and it became the nucleus of this religious center.

There are two suspension bridges spanning the

Approaching Rishikesh from the North

river, known as the Laxman and Ram Jhula. The Laxman Jhula was built in 1939 to replace the jute rope bridge that is believed to have been used by Laxman to cross the river when returning from Lanka. While crossing this bridge, you cannot help but notice the thirteen-storey high (!) Kailash Nand Mission Ashram (Swarg Niwas), or 'heavenly abode', founded by Sri 108 Swami

A simple but moving spectacle — the evening aarti

Kailash Nathji Maharaj. On the same side is the
Swarg Ashram — the splendid heartland of the
town with several ashrams, bathing ghats and
dharamshalas. Adjacent to this, at the head of the
Ram Jhula, is the Sivananda Ashram managed by
the Divine Life Society. Yoga and meditation
classes are held here daily.

Close by, and a little above, is the Yoga Niketan
Ashram which specialises in teaching Hatha Yoga.
Set in lovely gardens high above the river, this is
indeed a great place for meditation.

Returning to the West bank via the Ram Jhula,
you can visit the Bharat Mandir, dedicated to
Vishnu. There is a black idol made from a single
stone and the temple is believed to have been
established by the Adi Shankaracharya in the
ninth century. There are some interesting large
carvings of the other avatars of Vishnu on the
exterior walls.

At the Triveni Ghat nearby, there is an 'aarti'
performed every evening to Mother Ganga and it
is an extremely moving and beautiful spectacle.
Multi-tiered oil lamps cast a strong, warm glow,
reflected in the river that takes on a beaten silver
sheen in the setting sun. Individual prayers are
cast in small leaf-cups that hold flowers and a
single small flame, and bob prettily along with
the flow of the river, adding to this very special
experience.

Another popular ashram is that of Maharishi
Mahesh Yogi, based above Ved Niketan and
famed for the eighty-four artificial caves created
to live in. The ashram holds six-month courses
in meditation — it was the appeal of
transcendental meditation taught here, and the
influence of the Maharishi, that brought many
world famous personalities, including The
Beatles, here in the '60s ■

In Rishikesh, you must
not miss the spectacular
evening aarti held on the
banks of the river at dusk
— it is an evocative and
moving scene.

DAY 13
⏩ Drive back to Delhi via Haridwar

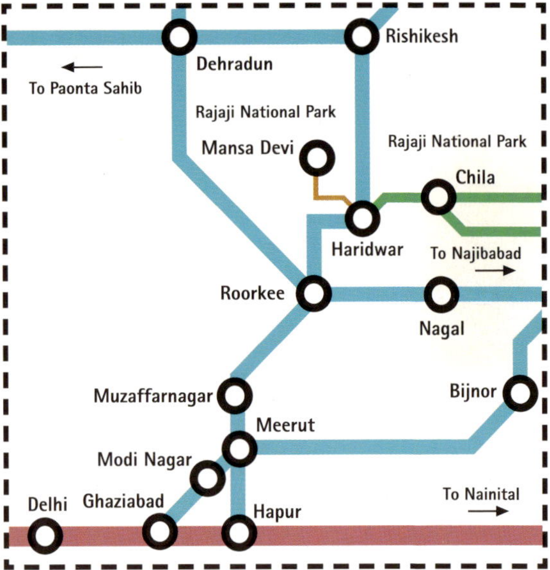

Rishikesh – Haridwar	25 km		Meerut – Modinagar	23 km
Haridwar – Roorkee	29 km		Modinagar – Ghaziabad	24 km
Roorkee – Muzaffarnagar	46 km		Ghaziabad – Delhi	19 km
Muzaffarnagar – Meerut	52 km			

In these holy towns, you are not allowed to partake non-vegetarian food, or alcohol — the sadhus recommend a very different route to reaching a higher plane!

Haridwar is only a 25km drive from Rishikesh. It is known equally by the names 'Haridwar' and 'Hardwar' since Shiva is 'Har' and Vishnu, 'Hari' and this is the gateway to the Gods' abode in the higher Himalayas. The pilgrimage route to both the Shiva temple of Kedarnath and the Vishnu temple of Badrinath is from here.

The great sage Kapila, is said to have spent time meditating here and in the distant past, this place was known as Kapilastan. It continues to be a favourite pilgrim spot for tens of thousands of Hindus who come for a dip in the Ganga at Har-ki-Pauri Ghat. This is supposed to be the precise spot

where the Ganga completes its descent from the mountains and meets the plains. There is a stone slab with a foot imprint believed to be that of Lord Vishnu. According to popular belief, he made an appearance here and blessed the assembly of gods and pilgrims. This ghat, which is jam-packed during the day, undergoes a dramatic change in character at sunset with a spectacular evening aarti performed on the banks of the Ganga.

Haridwar is one of the four pilgrim destinations where the Kumbh Mela is held every twelve years — the next one here is scheduled for 2010. A dip in the sacred river at this auspicious time is supposed to cleanse one of all worldly sins. The word kumbh means pitcher and the origins of this great event are steeped in mythology.

Colourful offerings — all that you need for your visit to the temple

THE KUMBH MELA

Aeons ago, the gods (devtas) and the demons (asuras) were locked in a battle of supremacy to control the Universe. The ocean was the repository of fourteen 'ratnas' or precious items. Most important of these was 'Amrit'; the nectar of immortality. After churning the ocean (Samudramanthan), for days on end, the precious nectar emerged in a pitcher and was grabbed by Jayant, the alert son of Indra. Accompanied by three others, he spirited away the coveted kumbh (or 'Amrit-kalash') but was chased by the asuras. There was a titanic clash between the two

Preparing for the aarti

opposing forces and to prevent the kumbh from being taken by the asuras, the precious nectar was secreted away at Haridwar, Allababad, Nasik and Ujjain. Finally, after a twelve day battle, the gods vanquished the asuras and were able to drink the nectar. According to another version, during the battle, four drops of nectar spilled from the kumbh and fell at these locations.

Yet another legend holds that the gods, in a pre-emptive move to prevent the powerful negative forces, the asuras, from forcibly taking possession of the kumbh, entrusted it to the devtas Brahaspati, Surya, Chandra and Shani. Learning of

Be careful while taking a dip in the river, the current can be extremely strong, so don't wade in too far.

this, the asuras chased these four for twelve days and nights during which the amrita was hidden in four places.

The Kumbh Mela is held every three years by rotation at the four centers. The most important Kumbh Mela is the one at the confluence of the Ganga, Yamuna and mythical Saraswati at Prayagaraj (near Allahabad) and the next one due here is in 2013.

The congregation at this mela is considered the single largest gathering of people for a specific purpose (religious or otherwise), anywhere in the world. Millions of people arrive for the Kumbh Mela from all parts of the country and a well-planned camp city is laid out on the banks of the river. The atmosphere here is mesmeric, deeply evocative and the visual impact leaves an indelible impression on the mind.

Ochre robes and bright saris mingle vividly on the sandy banks; brightly coloured shops spring up selling an intriguing assortment of wares; enticing aromas from dhabas mingle with cleansing smoke from 'havan kunds' and the sounds of bhajans, kirtans and discourses can be heard over the chatter of people.

The mela lasts a month and there are various auspicious days for taking a dip, the most important of these being the first, on Makarsakranti (January 14th). Since even the timing of the dip is of great consequence, a schedule is carefully drawn up, based on hierarchy along the spiritual ladder.

Besides taking a dip, people carry back their own kumbh of water, considered 'amrit' dispensed by the gods.

Another place of mythological significance is the Daksheswara, or Daksha Mahadev, Mandir located at Kankhal 3km downstream from the town

There is no such thing as off season for Haridwar — devotees from all over the country throng the temples and ghats and carry back their own pitcher of 'amrit'.

Besides serving as the gateway to Himalayan heights, Haridwar is also the closest point from where you can visit the Rajaji National Park (11km away). The Park was established in 1966 and is named after C. Rajagopalachari, the only Indian to make it to the post of Governor General of India (1947-1950). The Park is best known for its large herds of wild elephants that inhabit and travel through the area. Unfortunately, a railway line runs along the periphery of the park and over the years there have been some unfortunate cases of trains running into elephants crossing the railway line. This park has fewer visitors than its larger and older sibling at Corbett. Accommodation is available at the Forest Rest House at Chilla, which lies only 9km from Haridwar. The Park was, till recently, home to a large community of nomadic 'gujjars' who have traditionally used the area for grazing their buffaloes and other cattle. After several clashes with forest officials and some fairly high level intervention, they have now been relocated outside the park. Besides elephants you are likely to spot deer, but the mighty tiger does not inhabit this area. Reservations for the Rest House here can be made through the KMVN / GMVN offices either in Delhi or Dehradun.

Hanuman bhakts in the forest!

center. This is believed to be the spot where Sati's father, Raja Daksha performed his yagya to which he deliberately did not invite Shiva, thereby causing Sati's self-immolation in protest and Shiva's consequent cosmic dance of death.

Around 5km up the river is a beautiful spot where the Sapt Rishi Ashram is located. According to legend, seven rishis were engaged in deep meditation for the good of humanity when the goddess Ganga came to earth. In order not to disturb these holy men sitting at seven different spots, Ganga split into seven streams here!

You can also visit the Mansa Devi Temple on the hill overlooking town by either trudging up 1.5km or taking the chair lift. Another chair lift takes you to the Chandi Devi Siddhpeeth located in a lush forest atop Neel Parbat.

Haridwar is famous for its ubiquitous 'panda' community who are a major bastion of the religious hierarchy in all pilgrim towns. They have an amazing system of records and the panda looking after a particular family (this is based on not only geographical location but intricacies of clan, caste and even sub-caste!) will quiz each visiting member and add signatures and details of the family members to his record of that family tree. These records have passed down through generations of the panda's family and provided you had pious ancestors making a pilgrimage to Haridwar, you could trace your family tree and even see signatures of an ancestor! Pandas refer to their clients as 'yajmans' and arrange pujas, last rites — even practical affairs like accommodation and sight seeing, all for a price ofcourse.

Some are extremely conversant with Hindu rituals, have studied the scriptures and can be a mine of information but if you are not interested in their services, their persistent efforts to 'capture you' can be very irritating. Overall, unless you are religiously inclined, it is best to give Haridwar a miss and visit Rishikesh which is smaller, less crowded and far more scenic.

From Haridwar, it is a 200km journey to Delhi and should not take more than four to five hours. The route takes you through the small cantonment town of Roorkee, bypassing Muzaffarnagar, to Khatauli and then on to the Meerut bypass and straight to Delhi. A good place for a break is the Chital Complex, located between Muzaffarnagar and Khatauli. The road surface is generally good but the traffic after Roorkee can be quite heavy and overtaking is not easy on this two-lane highway ■

It is absolutely fascinating to meet the panda in charge of your clan and check out the family tree in his records.

SUGGESTED ITINERARIES AND COSTS

ITINERARIES

THE HIMALAYAN ODYSSEY

Days	The Odyssey			Short n Sweet	Off the Beaten Track
01	Drive to Naukuchiyatal			"	"
02	Visit Mukteshwar/ Sat Tal			"	"
03	Nainital			"	"
04	Around Nainital – Drive to Ranikhet			"	"
05	Ranikhet			"	"
06/07	Ranikhet & around			"	"
08	To Jageshwar & Almora			"	"
09	Binsar, Baijnath & Kausani			"	"
10	To Auli			Corbett	Chaukori, Patal B'war, Gangolighat
11	Auli & around			Delhi	To Munsiyari
12	Auli & around			-	Narayanswamy Ashram, Dharchula
13	Badrinath & around			-	Dharchula
14	Badrinath & around			-	To Ranikhet
	OPTION-A	OPTION-B	OPTION-C		OPTION-A / OPTION-B
15	Ranikhet	Rishikesh	Okhimath		Corbett / Lohaghat, Champawat Ranikhet
16	Corbett	Delhi	Rishikesh/ Ranikhet		Delhi / Delhi
17	Delhi		Delhi		

FROM THE OTHER END OF THE SPECTRUM

DAYS	THE FULL MONTY	LUXURY ONLY	1 NIGHT OF NON-LUXURY
01	Lansdowne	Mussoorie	Mussoorie
02	Pauri	Mussoorie	Mussoorie
03	D'prayag, Chamba To Dhanaulti	Mussoorie + Lakhamandal	Chakrata
04	Uttarkashi & Harsil	Mussoorie + Dhanaulti	Mussoorie
05	Gangotri & back	Rishikesh	Mussoorie + Dehradun
06	Barkot	Rishikesh	Rishikesh
07	Hanol/Netwar/ Lakhamandal/Mussoorie	Haridwar/Delhi	Rishikesh
08	Mussoorie & around	Haridwar/Delhi	
09	Mussoorie & around		
10	Chakrata/Tiger Fall		
11	Chakrata- R'kesh Or Mussoorie		
12	Rishikesh		
13	Haridwar/Delhi		

TRIP COSTS

'THE HIMALAYAN ODYSSEY' — 10 DAYS

	LUXURY	ECONOMY	BUDGET
Stay	25,000	15,000	5,000
Eating	6,000	2,500	1,500
Transport* (1500km)	12,000**	6,000***	4,000****
Totals	43,000	23,500	10,500

Staying costs for the 'Off the Beaten Track' section would not exceed Rs. 1000/- per night and could be as low as 300/- per night.

In the 'Continuing on the Himalayan Odyssey' section rooms cost around Rs.1200/- a night; luxury accommodation is available only in Auli and Rishikesh.

'FROM THE OTHER END OF THE SPECTRUM'

	LUXURY	ECONOMY	BUDGET
Stay	20,000	10,000	5,000
Eating	7,000	3,000	2,000
Transport* (1750km)	14,000**	7,000***	5,000****
Totals	41,000	20,000	12,000

*	Subject to vagaries of fuel prices
**	For a hired air conditioned vehicle
***	Sharing the vehicle with one other couple
****	Sharing the vehicle with two other couples

TREKKING AND RAFTING

UTTARAKHAND is virtually a paradise for trekkers. There are over fifty options ranging from the short and easy to high altitude glacial excursions. Since it is beyond the purview of this book to explore all these, our resident expert, Krishnan Kutty has drawn up a list of his favourites. Kutty, as he is known, has trekked extensively and climbed high mountains in India as well as other parts of the world and is currently based in Ranikhet where he represents the National Outdoor Leadership School (NOLS) of the U.S.A. and runs courses for them. With his expertise and years of experience you can trust his picks to be the very best!

FROM MUNSIYARI

TREK TO MILAM GLACIER (12,103ft/3690m)

ROUTE ▶▶ Munsiyari ~ Lilam (3 hours) ~ Bugdiar (6 hours) ~ Rilkot (6 hours) ~ Burphu (6 hours) - Milam(4 hours)~ Burphu (4 hours) ~ Martoli (2 hours) - Bugdiar (8 hours) ~ Lilam(6 hours) ~ Munsiyari (3 hours).

This is a moderate to difficult trek which will take 8-10 days. The path is well laid out and maintained for a good part of the year due to the transportation of food and fuel for the Indo-Tibetan Border Police troops stationed at Lilam, Bugdiar, Rilkot and Milam. The route follows the Gori Ganga upstream till its origin, the Milam Glacier.

TREK TO KHALIA TOP (10,650ft/3247m)

ROUTE ▶▶ Drive 6km to Balati Bend and then it is a 3 hour steep uphill walk.

A moderate one-day trek that takes you through mixed forest of birch, oak and rhododendron. As you climb above the tree line, there are beautiful alpine meadows (bugyals), at the top. From this point, you have excellent views of Nanda Devi, Nanda Kot and Changuch to the West, and the Panchachuli peaks to the East.

FROM BAGESHWAR

PINDARI GLACIER (12,989ft/3960m)

ROUTE ▶▶ Drive to Song (38km). Then trek to Loharkhet (1 hour), Dhakuri (5 hours), Khati (3 hours), Dwali (5 hours), Phurkia (3 hours) and Zero Point (3 hours).

This trek rates as an easy to moderate one and should take you 7-8 days. If you decide to see the Sunderdhunga valley as well, you will have to add another 3-4 days. The route takes you through villages, forests of oak, birch and rhododendron and ends at the terminal moraine of the Pindari Glacier. You will enjoy spectacular and VERY close views of peaks like Nanda Khat, Changuch and Panwali Dwar.

NAMIK GLACIER (11,316ft/3450m)
ROUTE ▶▶ Drive to Liti village via Bharadi (approximately 50km). Then trek to Satgarh (1 hour), Gogina (4 hours) and Namik village (4 hours). You can extend this by a day and trek to see the Namik Glacier (4 hours).

Another easy to moderate trek, this one is for the shorter duration of 3-4 days. The area you will be climbing in is very quiet and remote and you will encounter very few trekkers on the way even though this is on a well established trail. The route takes you across the Ram Ganga River, a little before Namik village and from this glacier too you will get excellent views of Nanda Devi, Nanda Khat and Changuch.

FROM RANIKHET
PANDUKHOLI (approximately 9774ft/ 2980m)
ROUTE ▶▶ Drive to Dwarahat (32km), then turn towards Dunagiri Temple to reach Kukuchina (21km). The trek to Pandukholi (2 hours) begins from here.

This is an easy trek that you can do in one day. The well established trail passes through a forested area for a short distance before reaching the top. This is mostly an uphill walk but one is amply rewarded at the top by stunning views. There is a temple at the top with two rooms for pilgrims and a sadhu in residence for most of the year. Carry plenty of water as there is none available on the way or at the top.

FROM GWALDAM
ROOP KUND (16,495ft/5029m)
ROUTE ▶▶ Drive to Lohajung via Mandoli, (approximately 41km). Then trek to Wan (5 hours), Bedni Bugyal (6 hours), Bugubasa (5 hours) and Roop Kund (4 hours). You can return the same way or trek to Ghat (3 days) and drive out to Nandprayag.

This trek will take you 7-8 days and rates as an easy to moderate one. Bedni Bugyal is an alpine meadow at 11,000 ft and very beautiful. From here, one can get brilliant views of the Trishul and Nanda Ghunti peaks. There is an interesting legend that tells of how human skeletons ended up in Roop Kund.

ALI BUGYAL – BEDNI BUGYAL
ROUTE ▶▶ Drive to Lohajung via Mandoli, (approximately 41km). Then trek to Wan (5 hours), Ali Bugyal (6 hours), Bedni Bugyal (3 hours), back to Wan (4 hours) and Lohajung (5 hours).

If you want to do a shorter, 4-5 day trek but with the same degree of challenge, this is an ideal one though you only visit the alpine meadows of Ali and Bedni Bugyal. These rolling meadows are particularly beautiful in August when they are carpeted in wild flowers. Set against a backdrop of Trishul, they are really quite stunning. Camping is the only option at both these places.

FROM NANDPRAYAG

KUARI PASS (11,939ft/3640m)
ROUTE ▶▶ Drive to Ghat (approximately 25 km). Then trek to Ramni (3 hours), Jehenjipani (6 hours), Pana (5 hours), Dhakwani (6 hours), Kuari Pass (3 hours), Khulara (2 hours), Auli (9 hours). One can also go to Tapovan (9 hours) and then take a jeep to Joshimath.

This trek is also known as the Curzon Trail, named after Lord

An idyllic village surrounded by fields of buckwheat

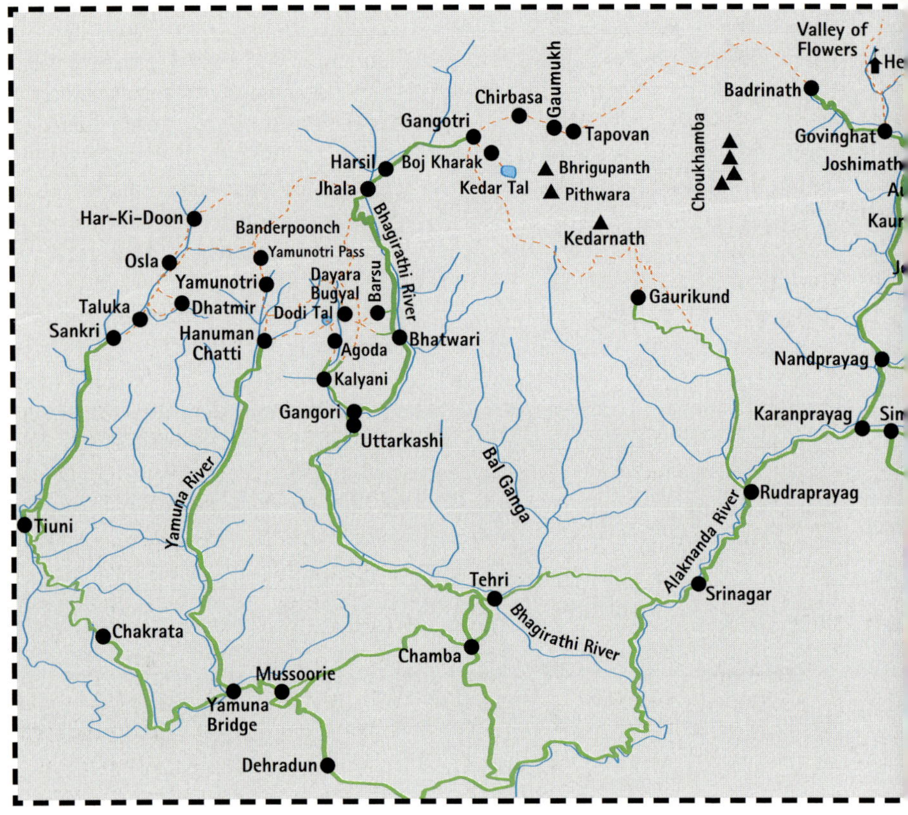

Curzon who attempted to visit it in 1905. It takes 10-11 days to negotiate and is a moderate to difficult route. The high peaks of Garhwal are seen from Kuari Pass, including peaks inside the Nanda Devi sanctuary.

FROM JOSHIMATH

HEMKUND SAHIB (14,199ft/4329m) & VALLEY OF FLOWERS (11,998ft/3658m to 12,995ft/3962m)

ROUTE ▶▶ Drive to Gobindghat (approximately 21km). Then trek to Ghangaria (5 hours). From here, one trail goes to Hemkund Sahib (4 hours) and the other to the Valley of Flowers (3 hours).

This is an easy to moderate trek that can be covered in 3-4 days. The Valley of Flowers is most beautiful from late July to September when the flowers are in full bloom and Hemkund Sahib is one of the holiest

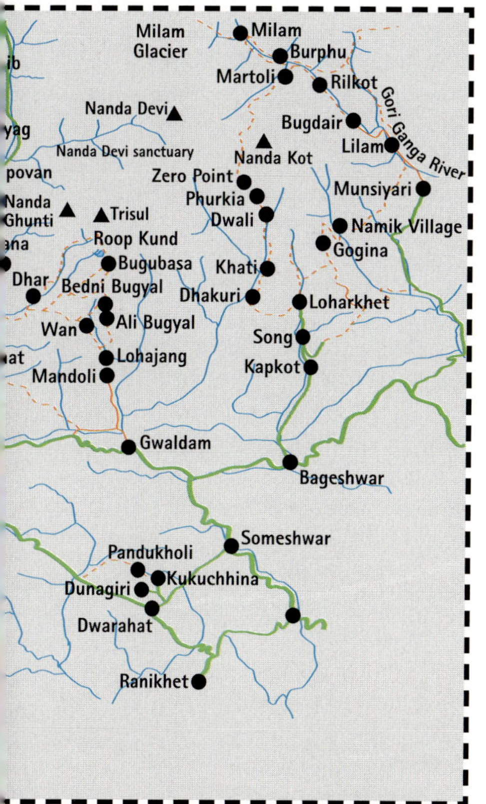

AUTHOR'S NOTE

Within these treks there are also some shorter two to three day options available. If you specify what you want to do, your tour guide can tailor-make a trekking itinerary to suit your preferences.

trek of easy to moderate intensity. You should be able to do this in 4-5 days. The Tons River flows through the Har-ki-Doon valley and you pass tall deodar trees, terraced mountain fields and forests of willows, chinars and chestnuts. The people of this area have the distinction of worshipping Duryodhan, the head of the Kaurava family. There is a fine temple dedicated to him at Osla. From Har-ki-Doon, one can also attempt to climb Jhandidhar Glacier (5 km trek) at 14,104ft/4300m. You can also trek to Yamunotri (29km), via the Yamunotri Pass (16,964ft/5172m).

of Sikh gurudwaras. Beautiful as it is, this tends to be a crowded route.

FROM DEHRADUN

HAR-KI-DOON (11,693ft/3565m) and **RUINSARA LAKE** (12,497ft/3810m)
ROUTE ▶▶ Drive via Chakrata to Sankri (approximately 150km). Then trek to Taluka, Dhatmir and Osla. From here you can take the trail to Har-ki-Doon or to Ruinsara Lake. This is a very popular and beautiful

FROM GANGOTRI

GAUMUKH (12,766ft/3892m)
ROUTE ▶▶ The trek goes through Chirbasa and Bhojbasa to reach Gaumukh.

The path to Gaumukh is a well travelled, easy to moderate, one that will take you 3-4 days. From the snout of the Gangotri Glacier flows the Bhagirathi River. This area is regarded as the origin of the river Ganga. One more day of difficult trekking will get you to Tapovan (14,629ft/4460m). This is a high alpine meadow with stunning views of the Bhagirathi and Chaukhamba peaks and Shivling.

KEDAR TAL (16,400ft/5000m)

ROUTE ▶▶ Up the gorge of the Kedar Ganga to Bhoj Kharak, Kedar Kharak and then on to the lake.

This is a trek of easy to moderate intensity that can be done in 2-3 days. It is 12km to Kedar Kharak, passing through some beautiful Himalayan birch forest en route. You can camp here and then make the steep (5km) ascent to the glacial lake surrounded by the high peaks of Meru (21,884ft/6672m), Pithwara (22,645ft/6904m) and Bhrigupanth (22,212ft/6772m).

FROM UTTARKASHI

DAYARA BUGYAL (9997ft/3048m)

ROUTE ▶▶ Drive towards Harsil. At Bhatwari (27 km), turn towards Barsu (9km). The trek to Dayara Bugyal (4 hours) begins from here.

This is an easy, one day trek. At an elevation of 3048 meters, Dayara Bugyal is a lush meadow with stunning views.

YAMUNOTRI (10,447ft/3185m) VIA DODI TAL (9862ft/3007m)

ROUTE ▶▶ From Uttarkashi, drive to Kalyani via Gangori (3km). Climb to Agoda (5km) and then Dodi Tal (16km), the Aineha Pass (6km) and then 22km down to Hanuman Chatti and up to Yamunotri.

The challenges of this trek are of the easy to moderate level and the route can be covered in 5-6 days. Agoda lies 450m above Kalyani and it is a short climb up with a camping site only 2km ahead. The next day is a 16km trek to Dodi Tal that is picturesquely set in a forest of pine and oak. The lake is the source of the Asi Ganga and is stocked with trout. There are great views of Banderpoonch (20,713ft/6315m) above the lake. Climb to Aineha Pass at 12,027ft/3667m and then descend 22km to Hanuman Chatti, the road head for Yamunotri.

Caution: Since most of these treks involve climbing above 10,000ft, acclimatisation is absolutely essential to avoid being hit by the dreaded AMS.

RAFTING

Rishikesh is now considered as the rafting capital of India. Actually almost all the camps that run the river are located on the river bank, 13 – 22km out of Rishikesh town, on the road leading to Devprayag and Badrinath. However, this degree of popularity brings many attendant problems — most notable being the crowding of the river and, according to some, the dilution of standards, as competition becomes fierce.

At the last count, there were close to twenty-five operators in action on the short 30km stretch of river where rafting is possible. This mushrooming competition has led to a price war and cutting corners leading to a deterioration in safety standards and levels of expertise of the river guides who steer you through the pulse-racing rapids. Since there have been some accidents, we recommend you pay that extra buck but ensure you are in the most experienced and safest hands available. The three listed below are veterans of the 1980s when the sport first started here and along with their wealth of

Krishnan at River Kali after crossing the Sin La pass

experience comes a respect for the river and its moods; they can give you an adrenalin filled trip without making any compromises! The rapids you will encounter on this stretch of river range between Grade I to IV and there are sections where you can bodysurf i.e. float on the river using the life jacket as a float. If it is your first time, pick the gentler section and graduate to the next level when you are comfortable.

Rafting season on the Ganga is between October and April only.

For those wishing to raft in May/June, the only option in Uttarakhand is on the Tons River. Himalayan River Runners operate on this tributary of the Yamuna and it is a beautiful place to visit, completely peaceful when compared with the action on the Ganga. The only disadvantage is that, compared to Rishikesh, it is quite a long haul from Delhi — it is a 140km drive from Mussoorie. However, if you are in the area, the rafting is thoroughly enjoyable and one can even cross into neighbouring Himachal and visit the Narkanda and Shimla areas, or drive on even further.

RECOMMENDED CAMPS

▸▸ *Himalayan River Runners* is steered by Yusuf Zaheer and his highly competent wife, Ganive. They also run a rafting camp on the Tons River in Uttarakhand and if you want high adventure, they can take you on the Zanskar River in Ladakh.

Himalayan River Runners, N-8, Green Park Main, 1st Floor, New Delhi-110 016
P: 91-11-26852602, 26968169/ 26854643 F: 91-11-26865604
E: riverrun@vsnl.com
W: www.hrrindia.com

▸▸ *Outdoor Adventures India* is run by a very competent team; Ajay Maira is ably assisted by the intrepid Pawan Sarao and this group also operates on the Zanskar River.

Outdoor Adventures India Pvt Ltd, S-234, Panchsheel Park, 2nd Floor, New Delhi-110 017
P: 011-26013571-2
E: oai@vsnl.com
W: www.raftindia.com

▸▸ Ajeet Bajaj heads another well known and reputed camp, *Snow Leopard*. They maintains high standards of safety and have a group of trained, experienced guides.

Snow Leopard Adventures Pvt Ltd., 9174, Sector C-9, Vasant Kunj, New Delhi-110 070
P: 011-26891473, 26134554
E: slaindia@vsnl.com
W: www.snowleopardadventures.com ■

THE ENVIRONMENT AND YOU

"Take nothing but pictures,
kill nothing but time,
leave nothing but footprints".

THE importance of respecting, preserving and not polluting the environment wherever we travel cannot be over-emphasised. Whenever we travel overseas we marvel at the cleanliness, the lack of litter, the absence of plastic/foil wrappers and so on. Yet within our own environs many travellers treat the roads, pathways, forests, meadows, streams and lakes as a dumping ground!

In many places the situation is so bad that the pristine beauty has been completely sullied. In this context the Rohtang Pass, (13500ft/4200m), above Manali in Himachal, comes foremost to one's mind — a group of school children went on a clean-up drive and could collect 25kg waste, in less than a hour, and built a 'garbage-man' on the snow field to bring home the point to spectators!

The tourist is not entirely to blame for the litter that greets us almost everywhere — the locals certainly do contribute. However, the onus falls on us to set the standard and certainly not make things worse.

Over the years some of the basics that one has followed are outlined below. Unlike the rest of the book, which offers suggestions, I would like to urge you to strictly adhere to some rules, (and ensure that your co-travellers do the same), so you leave the environment you came to see as beautiful and well-preserved, as it should be.

Carry a waste bag in each vehicle. Eating and drinking is an essential part of any road journey, but all empty packets, bottles, cans etc. need to be kept in the vehicle. Get rid of the bag when you reach your destination, (provided disposal facilities are available there), or in a garbage dump en route.

While walking through the forest, munching a chocolate or a biscuit, put the wrapper in your pocket and get rid of it later.

Apply the same rule while enjoying a drink and that great packed lunch by a rushing stream or a lovely meadow dotted with daisies.

If you are a smoker be extremely careful with cigarette butts as this is the cause of many an unintended forest fire.

Strongly discourage scribbling on trees, walls and buildings — we don't need to see cupid signs on every bench! Let the Himalayas make their impression on you and not the reverse!

Try to avoid blasting music while driving or picnicking.

For those who are going to be camping overnight, care has to be taken to ensure the use of kerosene or gas for cooking; toilet facilities

should be away from a water source; combustible waste such as paper, plastic pouches etc. should be burned; bio-degradable items such as food, unlined cartons etc. should be buried; while non bio-degradables need to be carried back. While using a stream, or lake, for bathing minimise use of soap and washing of clothes with strong detergents.

While visiting temples or gompas, shorts, skirts and tight-fitting clothes should be avoided. Shoes need to be removed and avoid touching religious books or relics.

In many places it is advisable to ask permission before taking a photograph of the locals; in some areas the camera is believed to capture the soul of the subject and photographs are a strict no-no.

Burn it, bury it or carry it out – be the invisible traveller! This is the best tribute you can pay the Himalayas ■

STAYING AND EATING RECOMMENDATIONS

THERE is an extensive network of Tourist Bungalows set up by Kumaon Mandal Vikas Nigam (KMVN) and Garhwal Mandal Vikas Nigam (GMVN) throughout the state. They have properties, both large and small, in almost every developed tourist destination. These are usually well located, have reasonably clean but basic rooms and the standard of food is quite good even though the variety limited. The only problem you may encounter is that the service is not always up to the mark – there is a typical lackadaisical 'sarkari' attitude to things. All the same, they provide good value for money.

A peculiarity of Uttarakhand is the paucity of 'good' accommodation in a large chunk of the state – the Garhwal region. Here with the exception of Dehradun, Mussoorie and Rishikesh, there are almost no private hotels of a remotely classy nature. If you don't want to rough it out, you will have to make your base in one of these towns thus limiting your choice of places to visit. Kumaon, on the other hand, has good private accommodation available in most places and it is very easy to find digs if you choose to visit the 'Lake District', Ranikhet, Binsar, Kausani – up to distant Auli, though strictly speaking this is part of Garhwal!

Hotels have been classified in various categories on the basis of tariff. We have, however, tried to provide some personal observations and you might at times find a C category hotel rated better than an A or B category.

A+	Rs.5000 + for a double room
A	Rs.3000 + for a double room
B	Rs.1500 + for a double room
C	Below Rs.1500

ALMORA
CATEGORY A+
▸▸ *Kalmatia Kala Sangam*: Located around 9km out of town on the road to Binsar, this is a lovely, exclusive property. Accommodation is in tastefully appointed cottages and the Continental food served here is the best you can get in the region. They also offer yoga, massages and acupressure. **P**: 05962-233625 / 231572; **E**: info@kalmatia-sangam.com **W**: www.kalmatia-sangam.com

CATEGORY B
▸▸ *Kasaar Jungle Resort* is located around 7km out of town on the road to Binsar. With 15 cottages set on four acres of land this is a good spot to put up your feet and relax. **P**: 05962-251127, 251181; **W**: www.kasaarjungleresort.com

CATEGORY B/C
▸▸ *Shikhar* is centrally located on the Mall, near the bus stand. It has suites, double rooms and singles to offer. **P**: 05962-230253 / 230395; **F**: 05962-231734

CATEGORY C
▸▸ *Deodar Resort* is a century-old bungalow owned by Richard Wheeler and offers very limited but peaceful accommodation in the hustle-bustle of Almora. **P**: 05962 - 233025 **E**: rwheeler@rediffmail.com

▸▸ *Savoy* is located above the GPO and has large airy rooms and a garden to sit out in. **P**: 05962-230329

▸▸ *Holiday Home* (KMVN) is conveniently located 2km from the bus stand in the heart of town. It has 7 cottages and 18 double rooms and a garden with good views. Contact KMVN for reservations.

AULI
CATEGORY B
▸▸ *Cliff Top Club* is the only resort on the meadow and its superb location

offers excellent snow views. Being an RCI affiliate, the rooms have small kitchenettes attached and the front rooms on higher floors are the best. The Indian cuisine here is very good and if affordable, this is the best place to stay. The only hitch is the extremely rocky drive up – the last 2km is quite a test for your car's suspension! **P**: 01389-223217 to 223220 or 05947-253232 to 253234
E: ctc_auli@mickyonline.com
W: www.ctcauli.com

CATEGORY C

▶▶ *GMVN Log Huts* are on a slope lower than Cliff Top and do not enjoy the same view but are well priced. They also have dormitories and regular rooms in the main block. Bookings are through the GMVN office. **P**: 01389-223208, 223305.

BINSAR

CATEGORY A

▶▶ *Club Mahindra Valley Resort* is outside the sanctuary area.
P: 05962-253028, 253062 & 253174
E: mahindraholiday@clubmahindra.com
W: www.clubmahindra.com

CATEGORY B

▶▶ *Mountain Resort*, Khali Estate is a prime property located within the sanctuary limits and one of the oldest in the area. Double storeyed stone cottages are set in a beautiful wooded expanse. Only vegetarian food is served but this is the place to stay in Binsar.
P: 05962-251011; **E**: mountainresort@rediff.com
W: www.resorthimalaya.com

CATEGORY C

▶▶ *Nanda Devi Tourist Rest House* (KMVN) is well located within the sanctuary and serves good food but the building is an unimaginative, ugly concrete block out of sync with its environment. **P**: 05962-280176

▶▶ *Binsar Retreat* has four tents in a spectacular location within the sanctuary.
P: 05962-280100, 09412092199
E: mailto:thebinsarretreat@yahoo.com / thebinsarretreat@yahoo.com
W: www.thebinsarretreat.com

BADRINATH
CATEGORY C

▶▶ *Hotel Devlok* (GMVN) is your best option here and has 10 deluxe and 20 double economy rooms. It is best to book well in advance during season or go to Auli for the night. **P**: 01381-22338
▶▶ *Hotel Narayan Palace* is another option and has 25 double rooms.
P: 01381-22380/81

BARKOT

▶▶ *Tourist Rest House* (GMVN)
P: 013752 - 24236

BHIMTAL
CATEGORY A

▶▶ *Country Inn* is set in beautifully manicured lawns and has comfortable rooms and all the mod-cons, including an indoor pool. However, it is located away from the lake and not for those for whom the lake-view is more important.
P: 05942-247120 to 22; **F**: 05942-247016
E: countryinn1@rediffmail.com.

CATEGORY B

▶▶ *Monolith Resorts* is a recently built resort designed by the well-known Delhi architect and author Gautam Bhatia (infamous for his delightful treatise on Delhi architecture, entitled *Punjabi Baroque*). Set above the lake, it enjoys a great overview of the lake. With cottages, a pool, and an amphitheatre, this is a good place to stay.
P: 05942-247415, 247582-3;

F: 05942-247581
W: www.monolithresorts.com.

▸▸ *Neelesh Inn* is also well located hotel and has 15 double rooms and 2 suites.
P: 05942-247117, 247080
E: unwindinc@hotmail.com

CATEGORY C

▸▸ *Pandava Tourist Rest House* (KMVN) has both cottages and regular rooms.
P: 05942-247005

CHAKRATA
CATEGORY C

▸▸ *Snow View Hotel*: This century-old building has been with the owner's family for over fifty years and is a charming colonial structure set in a rich forest. The eight suites are large and comfortable though a little basic, and the food is good.
P: 01360-272241/2, 272231, 272201
W: www.chakratasnowview.com

▸▸ *Himalayan Paradise* is affiliated to GMVN and on the way to Tiger Falls but is too far out of town.
P: 01360- 272252, 262525

▸▸ *Hotel Himgiri* & *Holiday Home* are both in the Sadar Bazaar area and are not a great choice. In a nutshell, *Snow View* is your best option!

CHAUKORI

▸▸ *Nandakot Tourist Rest House* (KMVN): This is superbly located, has both cottages and regular rooms and is the place to stay. **P**: 05964 - 244345

CHAMPAWAT
CATEGORY C

▸▸ *Chand Tourist Rest House* (KMVN): This has both regular rooms and dormitories. **P**: 05965 – 222030

▸▸ *Hotel Mount View* is the other option here. **P**: 05965 – 222220 / 222120

CORBETT
CATEGORY A

▸▸ *Country Inn Tree Tops*. Recently opened by the Country Inn group, this premium resort offers both rooms and cottages which are well spread over the property. They even have a tree top room, swimming pool and excellent conference facilities – the only thing missing is river frontage, but the overall ambience makes up for this.
P: 05947-284140-41, 09719293855
E: reservations@countryinnresorts.com
W: www.countryinn.co.in

Within the Park (CATEGORY B & C)

▸▸ *Khinnanauli, Gairal, Dhikala* and *Bijrani*, are the main Forest Rest Houses within the park area. Whereas Dhikala has the most accommodation, it tends to get pretty crowded and you would probably be better off staying at Khinnanauli (3 rooms) or Gairal (6 rooms). Although these rest houses do not provide the luxuries available in places outside the park, the atmosphere and much greater chances of spotting wildlife more than compensate. Bookings can be made through KMVN / GMVN or from the office of the director, Corbett Tiger Reserve, at Ramnagar
P: 05947 – 251489; **F**: 05947 – 251376

OUTSIDE THE PARK
CATEGORY A+ / A

▸▸ *Claridges Corbett Hideway* has cottages discreetly set in a mango grove, by the river. The food is good and though on the more expensive side, this is a popular place to stay.
P: 05947 – 251959 / 284132 / 284134
F: 05947 - 284133

▸▸ *Corbett Riverside Resort* has both suites and double rooms and is set along a stretch of the river. It offers a great

range of activities from riding and horse safaris to fishing and day treks and come evening, sitting around the bonfire to the sound of the river is a great way to unwind! They have recently opened a small exclusive resort — Corbett Jungle Hideaway — in the exquisite Sita Bani forest. **P**: 05947 – 284125 / 26; **F**: 05947 – 251960; Delhi **P**: 011-26560665 / 26565191
E: nainabahmad@yahoo.com
W: www.corbettriverside.com

CATEGORY B

▶▶ *Camp Corbett* (KMVN), besides regular accommodation they offer a one day package with all meals and a jeep safari thrown in.
P: 05947 -251225; **F**: 05947 – 253209

CATEGORY C

▶▶ *Camp Kyari* offers comfortable tented accommodation. Delhi **P**: 011-26850492 / 26963342; **F**: 011-26533212
E: wildrift@vsnl.com; **W**: www.wildrift.com

DHARCHULA

▶▶ *Tourist Rest House* (KMVN) is your best option here though there are a couple of hotels in town too.
P: 059672 - 22557

DIDIHAT

▶▶ *Tourist Rest House* (KMVN).
P: 059643 - 22234

DEHRADUN

The capital of the state has numerous staying options, but unless you have work here is not aparticularly great place for a holiday. Some options which offer a pleasant ambience are

CATEGORY A

▶▶ *Best Western Hotel Madhuban* is located on 10 acres of prime property on Rajpur Road. **P**: 0135-2749990-94
W: www.hotelmadhuban.com

CATEGORY A/B

▶▶ *Ajanta Continental* is also on Rajpur Road, and is not a large impersonal property — it has only 30 rooms.
P: 0135-2749595-98
E: hotelajanta@hotmail.com

CATEGORY B/C

▶▶ *President Hotel* is located close to the main market and is compact with 22 rooms. **P**: 0135-2657082/2652120
Delhi: 011-23714053-54

▶▶ *Shaheen Bagh* formerly a private residence is located around 15km out of town, off Rajpur road and has 4 comfortable rooms and a single room cottage. With 7 acres of land this is the most peaceful, relaxed spot to unwind.
P: 0120-2551963, 2524878
E: wildindiatours@vsnl.com

DHANAULTI

There are actually only four options in this sleepy, picturesque hamlet.

CATEGORY B

▶▶ *Drive-In, Dhanaulti* is the most expensive place in town but unfortunately only seven of their twenty-five rooms face the snow view. Rooms are modern and comfortable.
P: 01376 – 226225 / 26; **M**: 94-123-20056

CATEGORY C

▶▶ *Crown Plaza* is towards one end of the village, has comfortable rooms but the views are blocked by the deodar trees in front of it. **P**: 01376 – 226230;
E: intltdrs@del2.vsnl.net.in

▶▶ *Dhanaulti Retreat* was our preferred location. It is about a kilometer out of town towards Mussoorie and its comfortable but somewhat small rooms enjoy a good view. **P**: 01376 – 226233
Ghaziabad **P**: 0120 – 2710212, 2990628

▶▶ *Tourist Rest House* (GMVN)
P: 01376 - 226223

▸ *Tourist Rest House* (GMVN), is the option to the Forest Rest House and Log Cabins. **P**: 013772 - 22221

HARSIL

▸ *Tourist Rest House* (GMVN) is the only option and one that you will not regret. Although it has a convoluted drive in, and typical, basic accommodation, its location is superb, overlooking the river. Food is basic and if you carry supplementary supplies, you can really enjoy a scenic stay here. **P**: 013773 - 22210

HALDWANI

This is really not where you want to be – with the mountains just a couple of hours away! However, if you do have to make a stop here, your options are:

CATEGORY C

▸ *Hotel Saurabh Mountview*
P: 05946 – 222371/2; **E**: ssniryat@del2.vsnl.net.in

▸ *Hotel Nagpal Towers*
P: 05946 – 252395 / 252391; **F**: 05946 – 252281

▸ *Hotel Nanak*, run by the same group that owns Nanak Restaurant, popular and well reputed over the years for its good food. **P**: 05946 – 222775

▸ *Tourist Rest House* (KMVN)
P: 05946 – 222245

JILLING

'*Tashiding*', Jilling Estate is a delightful hideaway close to Padampuri, en route to Mukteshwar. It is a 2km walk (or pony/palki ride) up from the village of Matial to this exclusive estate set in dense forests where wildlife can still be seen. This is just the place for people who want to relax, soak in the mountain air, enjoy long walks and catch the snow views. The cottages are spread out among trees and there are no intruding TVs and phones to spoil a peaceful holiday! Run by an ex-IAF pilot Steve Lall and his family who call themselves "Practical Environmentalists & Nature Friendly Holiday Facilitators' – that says it all! **P**: 05942 – 246186; **M**: 94-123-83348 **W**: www.jilling.net

JOSHIMATH

▸ *Tourist Rest House* (GMVN) is a large accommodation with an old and new wing to choose from.
New Wing, **P**: 01389 – 222226
Old Wing **P**: 01389 – 222118

There are also several low priced private hotels in the market.

KAUSANI
CATEGORY B

▸ *Krishna Mount View* belongs to the same establishment that owns Krishna Hotel in Nainital and offers a range of rooms. **P**: 05962 – 263639,245022, 245008 **F**: 05962 – 245169; **E**: kumaon@del3.vsnl.net.in **W**: www.kumaonindia.com

▸ *Chevron Mount Villa* opened only a year ago and offers the well established level of comfort and hospitality as its siblings in Nainital and Ranikhet.
P: 05962 – 258016; **E**: hotels@bol.net.in **W**: www.chevronhotels.com

▸ *Staywell Resort & Cottages* is located on the Baijnath road. **P**: 05962 -245133, 232277; **M**: 94-120-44250

CATEGORY C

▸ *Trishul Tourist Rest House* (KMVN) offers both cottages and regular rooms.
P: 05962 – 245006

▸ *Divya Darshan Ashray Resort*, adjacent to the tea gardens, has small cottages but great views. It is in a stand-alone setting.
P: 05962 – 2448133; **M**: 94-120-44250

LANSDOWNE
CATEGORY C
▶▶ *Fairy Dale Hotel* is a stately old building and is a peaceful, quiet place to stay. **P**: 01386 -262599, 262237 **M**: 94-120-81837; **E**: TheFairyDale@hotmail.com
▶▶ *Tourist Rest House* (GMVN) is just a short distance from the bus stand. **P**: 01386 – 262509

LOHAGHAT
▶▶ *Mayawati Tourist Rest House* (KMVN); **P**: 059653 - 224313

MORI
▶▶ *Himalayan River Runners* set up camp here in the Tons Valley during rafting season. Delhi **P**: 011-26852602, 26968169; **F**: 26865604; **E**: hrr@nde.vsnl.net.in **W**: www.hrrindia.com
▶▶ *Aquaterra Adventures*; Delhi **P**: 011-26292760; **M**: 98-111-03831

MUKTESHWAR
CATEGORY B
▶▶ *Mountain Trail* is located at Sargakhet, 5km before Mukteshwar. **P**: 05942 – 286040, 286240; Delhi **F**: 011 – 22720675 – 77; **E**: sales@mountaintrail.com **W**: www.mountaintrail.com
▶▶ *Krishna Orchard Resort* is a modern hotel with over 20 rooms, many of them with good mountain views. **P**: 05942-286292; **E**: kumaon@vsnl.com
CATEGORY C
▶▶ *Tourist Rest House* (KMVN) **P**: 05942 - 286263
▶▶ *Camp Purple* has tented accommodation on the ridge in Sargakhet. **P**: 05942 – 286299; Delhi **P**: 011-26850492, 26963342; **W**: www.wildrift.com
▶▶ *British Retreat* is a delightful two bedroom cottage with a lawn and great views. They also run a restaurant, so good food is a given. **P**: 09935332040, 09336119018; **E**: thebritishretreat @yahoo.com
▶▶ *Somerset Cottages* with 5 rooms is another quaint option. Booking can be made through Zice Holidays **P**: 0981057329; **W**: www.ziceholidays.com

MUNSIYARI
CATEGORY B/C
▶▶ *Zara Resort* has 6 rooms and is the premium accommodation here. **P**: 059612 – 22524; Pithoragarh **P**: 05964 -224073, 226318; **F**: 225107; **E**: aksa_h@rediffmail.com; **W**: www.zararesort.com
▶▶ *Tourist Rest House* (KMVN) provides the biggest accommodation with regular rooms, 4-seaters and dormitories. **P**: 059612 – 22339
▶▶ *Wayfarers Mountain Resort* has huts and tented accommodation. **P**: 059612 – 22529

MUSSOORIE
There is a vast array of hotels to choose from, ranging from the very expensive to the more modestly priced. A listing is provided in the Appendix but some preferences are
CATEGORY B
▶▶ *Carlton Plaissance* (Carlton Hotel), is a beautiful building with an old-world charm. It is in a quieter part of town, on the road to the Academy and just after the turn off to Kempty Falls. The food and service is great and with its lovely gardens and snow views, this family run property is the perfect place to get away from the madding crowds! **P**: 0135 – 2632800; **M**: 93-581-20911 **E**: carltons@rediffmail.com **W**: www.geocities.com / carltonhotels.india
▶▶ *Kasmanda Palace* is located in a lofty spot above the Mall, almost half way up to Gun Hill. As the name

suggests, this was a palace and its grand rooms have all the modern comforts while retaining their stately character.
P: 0135 – 2632424, 2633949; F: 0135 - 2630007
E: Kasmanda@vsnl.com
▶▶ *Padmini Niwas* is a beautiful old building just below the Mall and besides the main block, rooms are spread along the hillside. P: 0135 – 2633023, 2632793;
E: harshada@nde.vsnl.net.in
▶▶ *Claridges Nabha Resort* is a little out of town, on the Barlowgunj Road.
P: 0135 – 2632525, 2631425
▶▶ *Dunsvirk Court* is located at the highest point around town and has grand views of the valley, the snow peaks and the township spread below it. The drive up is spine-tingling and the location superb. It is a large property and probably gets quite crowded during season.
P: 0135 – 2631043, 2632377, 2631669
▶▶ *Country Inn* offers a combination of 13 comfortable rooms and cottages that have been recently renovated.
P: 0135-2631190/94
E: reservations@countryinnresorts.com
W: www.countryinn.co.in
CATEGORY C
▶▶ *Garhwal Terrace*, (Tourist Rest House - GMVN) is on the Mall.
P: 0135 – 2632682, 2632683
▶▶ *Roselynn Estate*. P: 0135-263100

EATING OUT IN MUSSOORIE
The recommended hotels all have good restaurants and the Carlton has particularly good Indian cuisine. Other restaurants worth a visit are Four Seasons, Tavern and Le Chef to name a few.

NARENDRA NAGAR
CATEGORY A+
▶▶ *Ananda in the Himalayas* is an exclusive resort and spa – it won the Conde Nast Traveller Spa award for 2005. It offers a range of treatments, Vedanta classes and in keeping with its belief in holistic health it uses organically grown ingredients in its cuisine. P: 01378 – 227500; Delhi
P: 011-26899999; E: sales@anandaspa.com;
W: www.anandaspa.com

NAUKUCHIYATAL
CATEGORY B
▶▶ *Lake Resort* is probably the best property here as it faces the lake and yet is set back from it. It is spread over a large estate with a richly forested hillside at the back and rolling lawns in front. The rooms are comfortable and the food is good. Recently added facilities include a spa and gym so you can stay fit while indulging yourself at this beautiful property. P: 05942 – 247183/4, 247871
F: 05942- 247061; Delhi P: 011 – 26327731/2
E: lakeresort@sancharnet.in
W: www.naukuchiyatal.com
CATEGORY C
▶▶ *Parichay Resort* is run by KMVN and is well located, just before Lake Resort.
▶▶ Tourist Rest House (KMVN) is more basic and does not enjoy the same beautiful location as Parichay.
P: 05942 – 247138

NAINITAL
Hotels have mushroomed in and around Nainital at an exponential rate and currently the score is closing in on a hundred! A detailed list is provided in the Appendix but listed below are our recommendations.
CATEGORY A
▶▶ *Hotel Manu Maharani* is on the way to the High Court and you have a beautiful view of the lake from its

terrace. The rooms are comfortable and food very good. **P**: 05942 – 237341 – 8 **F**: 05942 – 237350; Delhi **P**: 011 – 23242446 **E**: manumaharani@vsnl.com

▸▸ *Claridges Naini Retreat* is another old property that enjoys a lofty location overlooking the lake. **P**: 05942 – 235105 **F**: 05942 – 235103; Delhi **P**: 011 – 26293905 **E**: retreat@del2.vsnl.net.in

CATEGORY B

▸▸ *Chevron Fairhavens* is a stately old building that was once the YMCA and the rich wood paneling adds to the ambience of the place. In keeping with the reputation this chain has built, the food is delicious. **P**: 05942 – 236057, 236604 **F**: 05942 – 236604; Delhi **P**: 011 – 22753151, 22758774; **E**: hotels@bol.net.in **W**: www.chevronhotels.com

▸▸ *Palace Belvedere* was the home of the Awagarh family and is now a beautiful heritage hotel. The rooms are spacious and comfortable and it offers great views of the lake. **P**: 05942 – 237434; **F**: 05942 – 235082; Delhi **P**: 011 – 26868992 **E**: belvederepalace@rediffmail.com **W**: www.welcomheritage.com

CATEGORY C

▸▸ *Sarovar Tourist Rest House* (KMVN); **P**: 05942 - 235570

▸▸ *Tallital Tourist Rest House* (KMVN); **P**: 05942 – 231985

Like Mussoorie, there are numerous good restaurants offering a variety of cuisines and the hotels recommended all boast of good kitchens. Some restaurants that you might want to try are, Gazebo, Machan and Embassy.

PANGOT

For those who want to stay a little out of town, surrounded by quiet natural environs and yet close enough to town to drive in for some action, Pangot, a

little out of Nainital is ideal. *Mountain Quail' Camp* here is run by a young enterprising couple and offers tented accommodation and a couple of rooms. The food is good and the atmosphere peaceful. **M**: 98-370-77537, 98-371-77537; **E**: blazeatrail@hotmail.com **W**: www.blazeatrailadventures.com

PATAL BHUVANESHWAR
CATEGORY C

▸▸ *Parvati Inn* is a recently opened hotel and a good place to stay. **P**: 05964 – 242312; Ranikhet **P**: 05966 – 220361, 220325

▸▸ *Tourist Rest House* (KMVN) **P**: 05964 – 242584. (There is another KMVN property coming up 13km further, at Gangolighat).

PAURI

▸▸ *Tourist Rest House* (GMVN) is very well located and has superb views of the snowy mountains. **P**: 01368 – 222359

RAMGARH
CATEGORY B & C

▸▸ *Cedar Lodge* is a small property set in an apple orchard. There are great views from here. **P**: 05942 – 281154; Delhi **M**: 98-115-15188; **F**: 011-26565191

▸▸ *Writers Bungalow* is part of the famous Neemrana chain and this is the place to stay if you are looking for peace, quiet and some old world charm and hospitality. **P**: 05942 – 281156, 281137; Delhi **P**: 24355214, 24356145 **E**: sales@neemranahotels.com; **W**: www.neemranahotels.com

▸▸ *Rose Mount View*, near the tea plantation, is set in five acres of apple, plum and apricot orchards. Although it offers only two suites, it is ideal for families with children as it has attached equipped kitchenettes. **P**: 05942 – 281139;

Delhi **P**: 011 – 23321427 / 0525

▶▶ *Hill View Tourist Rest House* (KMVN)
P: 05942 - 281155

RANIKHET

There is no dearth of accommodation here but we are listing only a few that we would like to recommend.

CATEGORY A

▶▶ *Windsor Lodge* is a recently opened hotel located in Kalika Estate, 6km out of town. There is nothing of the traditional hill architecture you might be hoping for but don't let the very built-up exterior get to you too much – this is the most up-market place to stay around here! The main wing has spectacular mountain views, but most of the rooms are contracted to a MNC. The rooms are all well appointed and some overlook the forest and golf course. What really puts this property on a pedestal is the superb cuisine – the restaurant offers an amazing choice and the Italian cuisine we've sampled there could put many a Delhi restaurant to shame! **P**: 05966 – 222098/99;
M: 094-111-97552
Delhi - **P**: 011-29521467; **M**: 98-100-13634
E: windsorlodge@email.com

CATEGORY B

▶▶ *Chevron Rosemount Hotel* is located in a quiet part of the Mall and is a lovely colonial bungalow set in a large garden with excellent snow views. Golfers will be happy to know that the hotel membership entitles them to play at the course in Kalika. The food is very good and we would certainly recommend this as a first option.
P: 05966 – 220989; **F**: 05966 – 2201391
Delhi **P**: 011 – 22753151, 22758774
E: hotels@bol.net.in
W: www.chevronhotels.com

▶▶ *Westview Hotel* is the 'doyen' of hotels in Ranikhet and in the old days was the only 'good' place to stay. Although in need of some attention, it has retained its atmosphere and charm. There are great sunset views here and the sprawling lawns are perfect to relax in. **P**: 05966 – 220261, 221075; **F**: 05066 – 220396; Delhi **P**: 011 – 26429790, 26425981

▶▶ *Holm Farm Heritage* is another wonderful estate located a little off the main circuit. It is a grand property with beautiful views. The road leading to it is a little rough in patches.
P: 05966 – 220891; **F**: 05966 – 220831;
E: holmfarm@rediffmail.com
W: www.holmfarmheritage.com

CATEGORY C

▶▶ *Ranikhet Club* was once the social hub of town with a grand wooden dance floor, brilliant library, courts, stupendous views et al. Unfortunately part of this beautiful building was ravaged by fire and the library entirely lost. The Chevron Group recently took over and renovated the Club and it has four small but comfortable rooms. Its location, atmosphere and the facilities available make this great value for money. You can book through Chevron or at 05966 - 220611.

▶▶ *Tourist Rest House* (KMVN): There are two in town and the one in the cantonment area is the larger of the two and offers executive rooms; **P**: 05966 – 220893. Monal, the second one, is conveniently located and offers only 5 regular rooms. **P**: 05966 – 221527.

Food at the hotels is good but we recommend Rosemount, the Ranikhet Club and Westview for both their Indian and Continental cuisine while Meghdoot, on the Mall, is well known for its Indian food.

RISHIKESH

There are two exclusive resorts, a little out of town and along the river that are certainly the best places to stay if they fit your budget.

Of course the town has a whole plethora of hotels to offer and there are also numerous tented rafting camps along the river, 13 to 22km out of town.

CATEGORY A+ & A

▶▶ *The Glass House* enjoys the most wonderful location along a bend in the river, close enough for the sound of its flow to lull you as you relax in the shade of fruit trees or take in a massage. Run by the Neemrana group, it is around 17km on the road to Devprayag and has large well appointed rooms.

P: 01378 – 269224, 269218
E: sales@neemranahotels.com
W: www.neemranahotels.com

▶▶ *Himalayan Hideaway* is just 2km before Glass House and is a new property set in a forested hillside above the river. Surrounded by trees and with the sound of the river welling up, this really is a perfect hideaway! The rooms are bright, airy and beautifully done and set as cottages. The food is wonderful as is the service and here too you can enjoy a relaxing massage.

P: 01378 – 261625, 261637
Delhi P: 011 – 26852602; F: 011- 26865604
E: riverrun@vsnl.com,
hideawayindia@hotmail.com
W: www.hrrindia.com

CATEGORY C

▶▶ *Tourist Rest House* (GMVN). Rishilok
P: 0135 – 2430373.

▶▶ *New Rest House* (on the by pass road); P: 0135 – 2433002

SITLA

Although this is not a listed destination, it is a possible excursion out of Mukteshwar or Ranikhet and is an ideal place to just chill out, walk in the forest and enjoy the mountain air.

▶▶ *Sitla Estate*, originally a family home, is set in a large property adjacent to the Sitla forest and overlooking the snowy peaks. It has four basic but comfortable rooms and you can't help but feel at home with the personalised care provided by its owner, Vikram Maira.

P: 05942 – 286030; P: 05942 – 286330;
Delhi P: 011 – 26241864;
E: maira@mantraonline.com;
W: www.sitlaestate.com

SAT TAL

CATEGORY C

▶▶ *Tourist Rest House* (KMVN)
P: 05942 - 247047

▶▶ *Wildrift Sat Tal Camp* provides tented accommodation. Delhi P: 011 – 26850492, 26963342; F: 011 – 26533212
E: wildrift@vsnl.com; W: www.wildrift.com

UTTARKASHI

The owners of Carlton Hotel in Mussoorie are opening the *Carlton Beach Resort* out of Uttarkashi and before the Maneri Dam. P: 0135 – 2632800
M: 93-581-20911; E: carltons@rediffmail.com

CATEGORY B

▶▶ *Shikhar Nature Resort* is located 5km out of town on the banks of the Bhagirathi, in Ganeshpur village. It has tented accommodation.

P: 01374 – 223762; W: www.shikhar.com

CATEGORY C

▶▶ *Hotel Shivom* is on the Gangotri road.
P: 01374 – 222328

▶▶ *Tourist Rest House* (GMVN)
P: 01374 – 222222, 222271 ■

NEW GETAWAYS

Fortunately destinations do not change – the same however cannot be said of staying and eating options. You now see entire hillsides being colonized by developers building cottages and multi–storied apartment complexes but you also see new resorts that have come up and some of these are in really good taste so here are some new places to look out for:

RANIKHET AND AROUND
DUNAGIRI RETREAT (A+)

▶▶ Nestled in the hillside is this charming nature resort. Located 45 km from Ranikhet it is far away from the general hustle bustle and the organic vegetarian food adds to the feeling of really 'getting away'.

P: 09810267719;

W: www.dunagiri.com

MERIGOLD COTTAGE (A)

▶▶ A quiet and peaceful retreat with eight rooms, lovely views, lots of sun and good food. Conveniently accessible from Ranikhet, it is 9km from the town on the road to Almora.

P: 05966-240185, 09810112973, 011-24358051;

W: www.merigoldcottage.com

RANIKHET GRAND (B)

▶▶ A new edition for the budget traveller this is conveniently located in the Ranikhet market. Many of the rooms have mountain views.

P: 05966-221144;

W: www.ranikhetgrand.com

VALLEY VIEW VILLA (A)

▶▶ This beautifully appointed pretty villa owned by Sabrina Singh is truly a home away from home! On offer are six comfortable rooms, a cute little café and all the basic facilities.

P: 05966-240266, 09412093826;

E: sabrinasingh5@gmail.com

SITLA AND AROUND
BOB'S PLACE (A)

▶▶ Located 14km from Mukteshwar, in Nathuakhan, this charming and cozy hideaway is the perfect place to put your feet up and relax.

P: 05942-285510, 09811034861;

E: bobanand@gmail.com

PINNACLES RETREAT (A+)

▶▶ Set within an orchard full of fruit trees and surrounded by forest of oak and rhododendron, this place offers you a choice of tented accommodation as well as a cottage.

P: 09313310640;

W: www.clifftopclubauli.com

HIMALAYAN VILLAGE, SONAPANI (B)

▶▶ Hidden deep within a rich natural forest this peaceful little getaway at Sonapani is ideal for those looking for some restful time.

P: 08006300100;

E: ashish@himalayanvillage.com

W: http://www.himalayanvillage.com/

NANITAL AND AROUND
ABBOTSFORD (A)

▶▶ A classic mountain house, with spacious rooms and a well–stocked library of new and old literature.

P: 011-29551191, 05942-236188;

E: abbotsfordnainital@yahoo.com;

W: www.abbotsford.in

CASA NANITAL (A+)

▶▶ An initiative of the Casa Group, Goa this property promises to live up to the group's stellar reputation and provide a luxurious escape in Nanital. It is expected to open in July.

GEORGES (B)

▶▶ Is a family run small hotel just half a kilometer before Bhowali. The tastefully done rooms and relaxed atmosphere make this a great place to stay when in this area.

W: www.euttaranchal.com/hotels/georges-bhowali.php

THE GARDEN VALLEY RESORT (A)

▶▶ Just 15 km from Nanital in Nighlat Village is this charming place with beautiful gardens spreading down to the river. It has well appointed rooms as well as a cottage and their food is legendary in this part of Kumaon.

P: 05942-220079, 09873099864;

W: www.gardenvalleyresort.com

THE LAKE VILLAGE (A+)

▶▶ A comfortable and pleasant resort on the banks of the Naukuchiatal Lake, this has spacious rooms with lake views.

P: 08006660205;

W: www.thelakevillage.com

2 CHIMNEYS (A)

▶▶ Strategically located in Gethia, a small village en route to Nainital, this beautiful cottage with brilliant décor has four suites and three rooms. Situated as it is, 2 Chimneys is great to escape to during the monsoon and winter months.

P: 05942-224541, 011-24321620, 08859969719;

E: 2chimneys@gmail.com;

W: www.twochimneysgethia.com

BINSAR

MARY BUDDEN ESTATE (A+)

▶▶ Located in the heart of the Binsar Wildlife Sanctuary, the Mary Budden Estate is a magnificently done property set in beautiful environs and targets the well–heeled traveller who enjoys understated luxury.

P: 09810185101;

E: contact@marybuddenestate.in

W: www.marybuddenestate.in

NANDADEVI ESTATE (A+)

▶▶ For those who enjoy communing with nature this is a great destination. It is a lovely colonial bungalow set in a twenty–acre estate in the core area of the Binsar Wildlife Sanctuary.

P: 08006658964;

E: Mukti@nandadevi.in;

W: www.nandadevi.in

CORBETT

TARANGI (A+)

▶▶ This resort boasts great views of the river, has beautifully done rooms and is known for its delicious food.

P: 09758822700;

W: www.tarangi.com

TIGER CAMP (A)

▶▶ Tiger Camp has a very nice natural feel with cottages offering

Staying and Eating Recommendations

comfortable accommodation without denting your wallet significantly.

P: 09811704651;

W: www.tiger-camp.com

LANDOUR, MUSSOORIE

▸▸ ROKEBY MANOR (A+)

This stately property with a rich history lies in the midst of a lovely forest, has great views and is a peaceful pleasant place to be in.

P: 0135-2635604, 2535605;

P: reservations@rokebymanor.com;

W: www.rokebymanor.com

HALDWANI

LEMON PARK HOTEL (A)

▸▸ This is a clean, modern budget hotel and is a comfortable place to base yourself in Haldwani.

W: www.lemonparkhotel.in

SAT TAL

COUNTRY INN (A+)

▸▸ Country Inn is the only up–market hotel in Sat Tal. It is a large property offering numerous rooms with pleasant décor and all the necessary facilities.

P: 011-46190100;

W: www.countryinn.in/contact_us.html

EATING

The food map has undergone a sea change with numerous small cafes, bakeries mushrooming on the hillsides.

BROWNIES

This is the most happening bakery in this neck of the woods (or should I say hills!). They have great chicken patties, bread and pastries. Their two branches are at Bhimtal and Haldwani.

P: Haldwani: 05946-320706, Bhimtal: 09411162835

PIZZA BITE

A cozy place to stop for delicious home made fresh pizzas and some fusion pasta! They have two outlets; at Haldwani and on the main road at Kathgodam.

P: Kathgodam: 05946-313725, 313726

W: www.pizzabite.co.in

CHAYYA

Located just before Gaggar Pass, enroute to Ramgarh, this delightful café run by the one and only Bunny Sahai, is a 'must stop' for all of you traversing this route. Its only 10km from Bhowali so if you have the time and yearn for greater heights you should definitely visit it—Chayya is at almost 7000ft!

WHAT TO CARRY

FOOD

Basic food is available throughout these routes and is usually good and wholesome though it can be boringly repetitive. Some bigger towns like Nainital, Mussoorie, Dehradun and Ranikhet have well stocked markets where you can pick up supplemental goodies; canned as well as ready-to-eat tetra packs are available. These towns also have some variety in the cuisine offered at the hotels and restaurants.

However, the more exotic food items you might want to indulge yourself with should be carried from your home.

DRINKS

Liquor is available but is comparatively expensive due to high taxes. The usual range of Indian made liquor, and of course the old faithful – 'Old Monk', and a variety of beers, is very easily available. However in view of the high cost of liquor licences coupled with seasonality most hotels Do Not have bar facilities. So carry your own liquor for your sun downer!

Bottled water and cold drinks can be bought in most places.

CLOTHING

Warm clothes to cope with very cold conditions albeit for short periods are a must, as also warm socks and sensible walking shoes. Ideally one should dress in layers so that you can add or shed as the conditions dictate – for a fair part of the day a cotton shirt will be enough as the sun is quite strong.

If you are travelling during the period between July to September, remember to carry some rain gear.

Headgear as protection from the extremely hot sun as well as dark glasses and sunscreen as protection against high UV rays is recommended.

MEDICINES

There are plenty of chemists in the main towns but you should carry a small stock of essentials including Paracetemol, Combiflam, your choice of medicine for stomach upsets, motion sickness, a good broad spectrum antibiotic for chest infections, something for a fever and muscle pull/pains, antiseptic cream and bandaids for minor cuts.

GENERAL

Binoculars and cameras are essential – film is available in the towns. Carrying your own sleeping bag is a good back up in the smaller places where accommodation is basic. A good quality, 1-ltr thermos – or even two – would come in really handy for that hot cup of tea/coffee you want to enjoy in scenic quietitude.

In fact, with one enthusiastic 'foodie' on board our car, we even carried a compact Korean stove (comes in a convenient rectangular shape; compact and easy to pack, it is fitted with an aerosol-type gas canister and available in our markets)! If you decide to follow suit, remember you can only do so if no air travel is involved.

Another useful little item is the hand sanitiser that lets you clean hands without water – like an anti-bacterial rub – and great when you are on the move!

A small torch and a Swiss Army knife and a car inverter will definitely come handy ■

DRIVING TIPS

SOME PRECAUTIONS THAT MAY PROVE VERY USEFUL

▶▶ If you are driving your own car, switching to tubeless tyres is strongly recommended. Both road conditions and new cars today make it possible to reach a speed of 100 kmph, and more, on some stretches. A front tyre blowing out, in such situations, could mean very serious trouble. Tubeless tyres have the twin advantage of deflating slowly and being capable of inflation that would allow you to drive up to 60km or more till you reach a repair shop.

▶▶ One should also carry a do-it-yourself repair kit. This is a very handy, if not necessary accessory to carry as small towns are not yet familiar with tubeless technology. A small air pump that plugs into the cigarette lighter socket is also available and, depending on the type, costs between Rs. 2000 and 6000.

▶▶ Carrying an additional spare tyre may seem a little extreme, but if you are not using tubeless tyres, can be very useful when travelling in remote terrain where one may not come across an air pump or repair shop for several hours at a stretch.

▶▶ Also carry a couple of spare tubes as the specific one for your vehicle may not be available everywhere.

▶▶ If you have a luggage carrier, add a 20litre jerry can of addition fuel as a contingency measure — sometimes all does not go according to plan and the scheduled refuelling stop could be dry.

▶▶ Carry spare engine belts, if your car still uses them, as also clutch and accelerator cables.

▶▶ A charger that plugs into the cigarette lighter socket is extremely useful for charging cameras and cell phones while on the move.

Above all, remember that in the tourist season there are a large number of inexperienced drivers from the plains hitting the hill roads and not conversant, or comfortable with 'hill-driving-norms' — so be cautious, and take those curves carefully ■

TRAVEL AND TOUR OPERATORS

UNLIKE Sikkim and Ladakh where there are good local tour operators, the vast majority in Uttarakhand are small hole-in-the-wall operators and not very reliable. The best option is to work with someone based in Delhi. However, for those visiting the Kumaon region, we do have one recommendation—particularly if you are planning a bit of trekking.

RANIKHET/NAINITAL

▶▶ *Himalayan Wanderers*, Northam House, Mall Road, Ranikhet
P: 05966-220626, 094-120-92702
E: aks_hay@yahoo.com
W: www.himalayanwanderers.com
Contact Akshay Shah in Ranikhet.

DELHI

▶▶ *Ibex Expeditions*, run by Mandip (Mandy) Soin and his wife Anita, this personalised, knowledgeable service is difficult to beat. Mandip is a climber and the benefit of his personal experience in planning a trek or even a simple holiday is of great help. Having been in the business for twenty-five years, they have seen it, done it and can handle things to perfection (Steam pudding served for dessert on a walk at 15,000 ft!!)
G-66, East of Kailash,
New Delhi- 110065
P: 011-26912641 F: 011-26846403
E: ibex@nde.vsnl.net.in
W: www.ibexexpeditions.com
▶▶ *Himalayan River Runners* is steered by Yusuf Zaheer and his highly competent wife, Ganeve. They also run a rafting camp on the Tons River in Uttarakhand and if you want high adventure, they can take you on the Zanskar River in Ladakh.
N-8, Green Park Main, 1st Floor,
New Delhi-110 016
P: 011-26852602, 26968169 and 26854643 F: 011-26865604
E: riverrun@vsnl.com
W: www.hrrindia.com
▶▶ *Shikhar International (P) Ltd*, 209 Competent House
F-14 Middle Circle,
Connaught Place, New Delhi.
P: 011- 23312444, 23312666
F: 011-23323660
W: www.himalayanhillstation.com
▶▶ The Big Boys a.k.a. *Travel Corporation of India*, Sita World Travels, Cox and King and others. The advantage is that they probably operate in the city you live in, and are therefore more accessible. However, in this age of communication by e-mail and low STD tariffs, this advantage isn't necessarily a key issue. Does size matter? Maybe. Particularly if you make up your mind at the last minute to take off somewhere and bookings in the hotel you want to stay in and/or air tickets aren't available. They may have the clout

to make things happen, when others have given you the thumbs down.

BANGALORE

▸▸ *Hammock Leisure Holiday Pvt. Ltd.* was set up to 10 years ago by a group of young professionals from the service industry. With branches in Cochin and Mumbai and associate office in Chennai they are well placed to customise your holiday.
314/1 Vijay Kiran
7th Cross,
Domlur Layout
Bangalore.
P: 25351877/25351444
E: hammock@vsnl.net
W: www.hammockholidays.com ■

A BIG advantage of travelling in this state is the easy availability of reasonably good medical facilities in comparison with some of the other, more remote mountainous regions.

For the road traveller, there are decent hospitals and nursing homes in Haldwani, Nainital, Ranikhet, and Almora in the Kumaon belt and in Dehradun, Haridwar, Rishikesh and Mussoorie on the Garhwal side. In the other areas, there are Civil Hospitals at all district headquarters and barring a serious condition, there is sufficient help available and little to worry about. There are also plenty of chemists in most towns, so even if you have forgotten your medical kit, you can make one up on the move ■

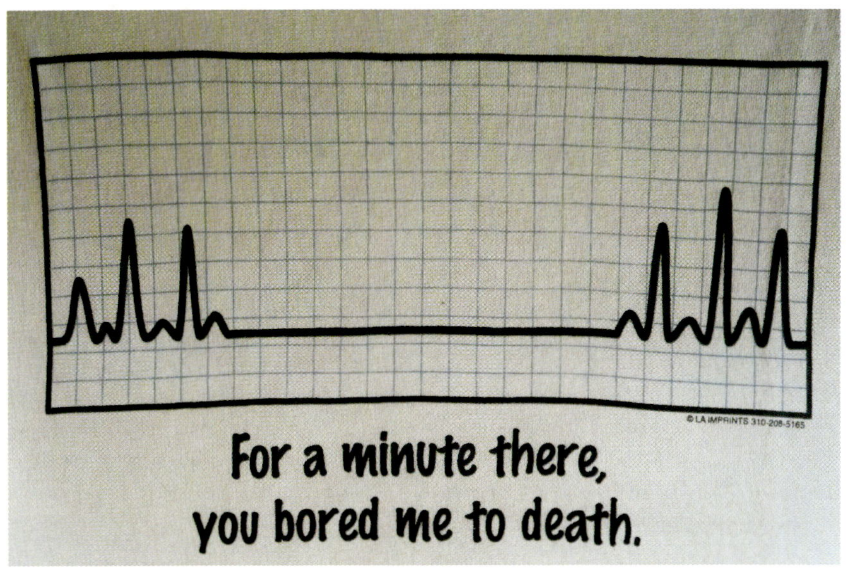

GMVN AND KMVN OFFICES

GMVN

GMVN

DEHRADUN
G.M. (Touism) GMVN Ltd. 74/1, Rajpur Road
P: 0135-2746817, 2747898, 2749308
F: 0135-23746847, 2743104, 2748478
E: gmvn@gmvnl.com, gmvn@sancharnet.in

Dona Travels
45 Gandhi Road, Dehradun-248 001
P: 0135-2653309, 2654371

RISHIKESH
Trekking and Mountaineering Division
Garhwal Mandal Vikas Nigam Ltd.
Muni-ki-Reti, Rishikesh-249 201
P: (0135) 2430799
F: (0135)2430372
E: yatra@gmvnl.com, yatraoffice@sancharnet.in

A.G.M. (T), GMVN Ltd.
Yatra Office, Modern Reception Center
(Advance Reservation Center) Shail Vihar
Haridwar by-pass Road, Rishikesh-249 201
P: 0135-2431793, 2431783, 2432648
F: 0135-2430372
E: yatra@gmvnl.com
yatraoffice@sancharnet.in

NEW DELHI
PRO, GMVN, 102 1ST Floor, Indraprakash
21, Barakhamba Road, New Delhi-110 001
P: 011-23326620, 23350481
F: 011-23327713
E: gmvnl@bol.net.in

MUMBAI
PRO, GMVN, C/o MTDC, CDO Hutments
Madame Cama Road
P: 022-22024415, 22027762
F: 022-22024415, 22843197

CHENNAI
PRO, GMVN, C/o Tamil Nnadu Tourist Complex
Valzaha Road, Chennai-600 002
P: 044-25363542
E: Chennai@gmvnl.com

KOLKATA
PRO, GMVN, C/o "Marshall House"
Room No.224, 33/1, 2nd Floo,
Netaji Subhash Road
T: 033-22610554
E: prokolkatta@vsnl.net

BANGALORE
PRO, GMVN, 29/2, IInd floor
Nanjappa Mansion, K.H. Road, Shanti Nagar
Bangalore-560 027
P: 080-2249378

AHMEDABAD
PRO, GMVN, 301 Ashwamegh House,
Behind Choice Restaurant, Near Swastik Char
Rasta, Navrangpura, Ahmedabad-380 009
P: 079-6564245, 6421214

JAIPUR
PRO, GMVN, Govt. Hostel Campus
Opposite G.P.O.
M.I. Road, Jaipur-302 001
P: 0141-2378892

CHANDIGARH
PRO, GMVN, C/o U.P. Tourism, Room No.64
Sector-17 M, Chandigarh-160 017
P: 0172-2707649
F: 0172-2713988
E: chandigarh@gmvn.com

LUCKNOW
PRO, GMVN, Khushnuma Complex, Flat No.4-7
RF Bahadur Marg, Near State Guest House
P: 0522-2207844
E: lucknow@gmvnl.com

HARIDWAR
PRO, GMVN, Lalta Rao Bridge, Haridwar
P: 01334-224240
F: 01334-228686

KMVN

General Manager (Tourism) Touism Dev. Officer
Kumaon Mandal Vikas Nigam Ltd.
Oak Park House, Nainital-263001
P: 05942-236356; F: 05942-236897

FOR RESERVATION OF ACCOMMODATION

Manager Central Reservation Center T.R.H.
Sukhatal, Nainital – 263001
P: 05942-236374, 231436; F: 05942-236374

AHMEDABAD

PRO, KMVN, 301 Ashwamegh House
8/H Choice Restaurant, Near Swastik Char Rasta,
Navrangpura P: (079) 26421214

DEHRADUN

PRO, KMVN, 74/4, Rajpur Road, Dehradun
P: (0135) 2749720 F: (0135) 2746847

JAIPUR

PRO, KMVN, Hotel Tourism Campus
Govt. House, M.I. Road, Opp. G.P.O.
P: (0141)5124036

KOLKATA

PRO, KMVN, c/o U.P. Tourism, 12 A
Netaji Subhash Road, Kolkata-700 001
P: (033) 22207855 F: (033) 22206798

LUCKNOW

PRO, KMVN, 2 Gopal Khera House
Sarojini Naidu Marg. P: (0522) 2239434

MUMBAI

PRO, KMVN, C/o Core Communications
1B/404, Royal Sands, Next City Mall
New Link Road, Andheri (W)
P: (022) 26354588 / 26304880

NAINITAL

Manager, Parvat Tours, KMVN, Tallital
P: (05942) 235656 / 231504

NEW DELHI

PRO, KMVN, 103, 1st Floor, Indra Prakash
Building, 21, Barakhamba Road New Delhi-
110001 P: (91-011) 23712246, 51519366
F: (91-011) 23319835

APPENDIX

NAINITAL HOTELS

NAME OF HOTEL	TELEPHONE	FAX	TARIFF
Hotel Abhiruchi	232512		250-500
Hotel Ahujas	235561		300-1200
Alka "The Lake Side Hotel"	235220	236628	2300-3000-4500
Alpine Chalet	236254		2000/-
Hotel Ambassador	235642, 236825		400-750-1200
Hotel Anamika Ocean	235618, 235015		400-750-1200
Hotel Ankur Plaza	235448		500-1250
Hotel Archana	235884	235884	360-450, 600-1200
Hotel Arif Castles	236005	236231	2700-3100-3500
Armadale	235805, 235855	236205	900-1500, 2200-2800
Hotel Aroma	235354, 236824		600-1600
Ashok Hotel	235721		350-450, 550-750
Atithi Hotel	235080		(Contact Reception)
Balrampur House "Heritage Resort"	236236, 239902		1200-1800-2700
Basera	235885		300-1000
Belvedere Palace	235082	235082	1350-1890
Capri Hotel	235690		1000-1800
Hotel Channi Raja	235643		1550-2250
Hotel City Heart	235228, 239752		800-1400
Claridges Naini Retreat	235105, 235108	235103	2400-3600
Classic	235173	237704	1700-2200
Hotel Deep Jyoti	236934		300-500
Hotel Earlscourt	236381, 237128	237030	1500-2500
Hotel Elphinstone	235534		-
Evelyn Hotel	235457, 237457	236457	650-1400
Hotel Everest	235453		1200-1800-2200
Chevron Fairhavens	236057, 232972	236604	800-2200-3000
Grand Hotel	235406	237057	1500-1800
Hotel Gurdeep	235528		400-2200
Himalaya Hotels	235258, 235587		500-850, 750-850
India Hotel	235517, 239017		700-1200
Jagati Hotel	239686		350-450-550
Kalpana Hotel	236357, 236530		450/-
Kohli Hotel	236368		400/-
Krishna Hotel	231646, 231639	237550	1000-1400
Lakeside Inn	235777	236827	1000-1150-2350
Hotel Lalit	236394	238774	250-500
Hotel Langdale Manor	235447	231362	1220-1370-1620
Hotel Maharaja	235281		350-450
Hotel Meghdoot	235124		-
The Manu Maharani		237350	3300-4500-5200
Hotel Mansarovar	235581		350-850
Hotel Metropole	235589, 236343	236379	1200-1400-1600
Hotel NainiVision	235496		200-650
Nanak Hotel	239047		250/- onwards
National Hotel	235537		-
Hotel Nepoli	235090		-
Hotel New Pavillion	236178		450-1200
Hotel Oak Shade	235672		-
The Palace Resort	236065, 236950	237190	1195-1995

NAME OF HOTEL	TELEPHONE	FAX	TARIFF
Hotel Palace	235125, 235521		600-1800
Hotel Paryatak	235815		-
Hotel Payal	235248		300-450
Hotel Prashant	235347		300-1000
Hotel Pratap Regency	235865-66		550-1050-1250
Hotel Prince	236817		695-1195
Ratan Jyoti	236105		800-1200
Regency Gopaltara	235356		500-1500
Royal Hotel	236007, 235357	235357	1600-2100
Sarovar Hotel	231382		500/-
Savoy Hotel	235721		250-400-550-800
Shalimar Hotel	235432, 237176	235493	600-800
Shervani Hilltop Inn	236128	236304	2400-2600
Hotel Sheela	235194		200-600
Hotel Shiv Raj	235698		250/- onwards
Hotel Silverton	235249	235493	800-900-1150
Sita Kiran	237054	235323	500/-
Standard Hotel	235602		200-350
Swiss Hotel	236013, 235972	235493	2000/-
Tourist Rest House, Sukhatal	235400		1500-1500-800
Tourist Rest House, Tallital	235570		2000-2000-1000
Tourist Rest House, Snow View	238570		600-600-300
Vikram Vintage Inn	236177-79	236177-79	3000/-
Hotel Vikrant	235031		-
Vinayak Hotel	236906		400-1000
Vimal Kunj	235433		450/-
Welcome Resort	235552, 236852	235493	1650/-

MUSSOORIE HOTELS

NAME OF HOTEL	LOCATION	TELEPHONE	FAX
A-CLASS			
Avlon Resorts (Gun Hill)	Kulri Bazar	2631698, 2632893	
Brent Wood	Kulri Bazar	2632126, 2632102	2632604
Connaught Castle	Kulri Bazar	2632210, 2631138	2632638
Drive Inn	Kulri Bazar	2631226, 2631227	2632555
Green Castle	Kulri Bazar	2632657, 2631461	
Kasmanda Palace	Kulri Bazar	2633949, 2632424	2630007
Pearl	Kulri Bazar	2631045, 2631046	
Star Regency	Kulri Bazar	9837054343	
Shipra	Kulri Bazar	2632494, 2632373	2632941
Classic Heights	Library (Gandhi Chowk)	2632514, 2632590	
Grace Mount	Library (Gandhi Chowk)	2632434, 2632534	
Oasis	Library (Gandhi Chowk)	2631001	
Padmini Niwas	Library (Gandhi Chowk)	2631093	2632793
Duns Virk Court	Library (Gandhi Chowk)	2631043, 2632377	2631669
JP Residency Manor	Mussoorie-Dehradun Road	2631800, 2631820	
Claridges Nabha Palace	Mussoorie-Dehradun Road	2631426, 2631427	2631425
Fort Resorts	Mussoorie-Dehradun Road	2631611, 2632728	2631127
Hardrock	Mussoorie-Dehradun Road	2361240	2631341

NAME OF HOTEL	LOCATION	TELEPHONE	FAX
B-CLASS			
Abhinandan	Kulri Bazar	2631888	
Apsara	Kulri Bazar	2632066	
Bikram	Kulri Bazar	2633630	
Charlene	Kulri Bazar	2632884, 2632808	
Garhwal Terrace	Kulri Bazar	2632682, 2632683	
Hamer International	Kulri Bazar	2632818	
Hill Queen	Kulri Bazar	2632238, 2632797	
Holiday Inn	Kulri Bazar	2632794, 2632225	
Honey Moon Inn	Kulri Bazar	2632378, 2631778	
Horizon	Kulri Bazar	2632899, 2630681	2631588
Howard Int.	Kulri Bazar	2632113, 2632093	
Mall Palace	Kulri Bazar	2632497, 2632097	2632297
Meedo Palace	Kulri Bazar	2632044, 2631111	
Mid Town	Kulri Bazar	2632856, 2632649	
Mussoorie Int.	Kulri Bazar	2632143, 2631243	
Neelam Int.	Kulri Bazar	2632195, 2632196	
Palki	Kulri Bazar	2632139	
Park	Kulri Bazar	2632336, 2631631	
Piknik	Kulri Bazar	2631150	
Pine Retreat	Kulri Bazar	2632513, 2631213	
Pioneer	Kulri Bazar	2632188	
Raj Deluxe	Kulri Bazar	2632338	
Rock Wood	Kulri Bazar	2632850, 2632418	
Royal Classic	Kulri Bazar	2631452, 2632152	
Samrat	Kulri Bazar	2632707, 2632156	
Singar	Kulri Bazar	2632170	
Shivam	Kulri Bazar	2632308	
Sunny Cot	Kulri Bazar	2632789	
Valley View	Kulri Bazar	2632324, 2632211	
Walnut Grovoe	Kulri Bazar	2631877, 2632311	
Lux Mount	Kulri Bazar	2631659	
Ashoka Cont.	Library (Gandhi Chowk)	2632490, 2631409	
Cloud End	Library (Gandhi Chowk)	2632242	
Dwaper	Library (Gandhi Chowk)	2632925, 2630825	
Highness Height	Library (Gandhi Chowk)	2631484	
India	Library (Gandhi Chowk)	2632359	
Lord's Mussoorie Club	Library (Gandhi Chowk)	2630200, 2630168	
Paramount	Library (Gandhi Chowk)	2632352, 2631352	
Prince	Library (Gandhi Chowk)	2631001	
Savoy	Library (Gandhi Chowk)	2632120, 2632010	
Shilton	Library (Gandhi Chowk)	2632983, 2631036	
Sterling Resorts	Library (Gandhi Chowk)	2631713, 2631712	
Sun N Snow	Library (Gandhi Chowk)	2632155, 2631255	
Sun N Star	Library (Gandhi Chowk)	2631311, 2630022	
Vishnu Palace	Library (Gandhi Chowk)	2632932, 2632732	
Crystal Palace	Library (Gandhi Chowk)	2630858	
Monarch	Library (Gandhi Chowk)	2630303, 2630606	
Sun Rise	Library (Gandhi Chowk)	2631180	
Country Inn	Mussoorie-Dehradun Road	2631190, 2631194	
Sangrila Inn	Mussoorie-Dehradun Road	2631666	

NAME OF HOTEL	LOCATION	TELEPHONE	FAX
Solitair Plaza	Mussoorie-Dehradun Road	2632164, 2632165	
Vasant Palace	Mussoorie-Dehradun Road	2633881, 2633882	
Jass Resorts	Mussoorie-Dehradun Road	2632491, 2630704	
Ashiana	Camel's Back Road	2632945, 2631635	2630332
Deep Mountain View	Camel's Back Road	2632470, 2632070	
Filigree	Camel's Back Road	2632380, 2631380	2632360
Nand Residency	Camel's Back Road	2632088, 2631442	2631442
Pink Pavillion	Camel's Back Road	2632272	
Ashirwad	Landour Bazar	2631166, 2632915	2633152
Darpan	Landour Bazar	2631183, 2632483	
Golden Heaven	Landour Bazar	2633319, 2631134	
Himalaya Club	Landour Bazar	2632805	
Shiva Continental	Landour Bazar	2632175	2632780
Poornima	Landour Bazar	2632550	

NAME OF HOTEL	LOCATION	TELEPHONE
C-CLASS		
Amar	Kulri Bazar	2632183
Ashok Plaza	Kulri Bazar	2633452
Brite Star	Kulri Bazar	2631603
Clark	Kulri Bazar	2632393, 2631392
Doon Palace	Kulri Bazar	2632566
Everest	Kulri Bazar	2632954
Hakmans	Kulri Bazar	2632159
Hill View	Kulri Bazar	2632764
Mansarovar	Kulri Bazar	2632764
Minerva	Kulri Bazar	2632946
Raghushree	Kulri Bazar	2632287
Rama	Kulri Bazar	2632851
Regal	Kulri Bazar	2632133
Roxy	Kulri Bazar	2632741
Saraswati	Kulri Bazar	2631005
Sparsh	Kulri Bazar	2631220
Surya Kiran	Kulri Bazar	2631103
Tourist Home	Kulri Bazar	2631221
Vikas	Kulri Bazar	2632735
Raj Palace	Kulri Bazar	2633345
Atithi	Library (Gandhi Chowk)	2632351
Adarsh	Library (Gandhi Chowk)	2632345, 2632346
Ambica Palace	Library (Gandhi Chowk)	2631229, 2634229
Ambica Resorts	Library (Gandhi Chowk)	2632160
Goyal Palace	Library (Gandhi Chowk)	2632043
Green View	Library (Gandhi Chowk)	2631361
Gulmarg	Library (Gandhi Chowk)	2631113, 2630113
Imperial	Library (Gandhi Chowk)	2632632
Jeet	Library (Gandhi Chowk)	2632775, 2631131
Kahakashan	Library (Gandhi Chowk)	2633989
Laxmi Palace	Library (Gandhi Chowk)	2632774
Mall View	Library (Gandhi Chowk)	2632307, 2632407
Mayur	Library (Gandhi Chowk)	2632696

NAME OF HOTEL	LOCATION	TELEPHONE
Ratan	Library (Gandhi Chowk)	2632719, 2630719
Snow View	Library (Gandhi Chowk)	2630464
Whispring Windows	Library (Gandhi Chowk)	2632020, 2632611
Ever Green	Mussoorie-Dehradun Road	2632503, 2631503
Youth Hostel	Mussoorie-Dehradun Road	2630504
Carton Plaisance	LBSN Academy Road	2632800
Shalimar	LBSN Academy Road	2632410
Wild Flower House	LBSN Academy Road	2632900
Ajay	Camel's Back Road	2632648
Broadway	Camel's Back Road	2632243
Naveen	Camel's Back Road	2630779
Peak View	Camel's Back Road	2632052, 2632596
Summer Nest	Camel's Back Road	2632146, 2631346
Sheela Lodge	Camel's Back Road	2631667
Uday	Camel's Back Road	2631016
Nishima	Landour Bazar	2632227, 2630298
Regency	Landour Bazar	2631200
Surer	Landour Bazar	2632912, 2631972
Urvashi	Landour Bazar	2632194
Panjab Tourism	Landour Bazar	2632655

PAYING GUEST HOUSES AT MUSSOORIE

NAME	LOCATION	TELEPHONE
Bhagwanti Singhal	Kulri	2632047
Santosh Devi Raj Bhavan	Kempty Road	2630444, 2630012
Krishna Niwas	Bala Hisar	2630285
Ivy bank	Landour Cantt.	2631433, 2630278
Krishna Nivas	Camel's Back Road	2631609
Albani Lodge Estate	Near City Board	2732558
Kanak Building	Library	2632942
Raghuvir Singh	Near Sapling Estate	-
Pushpa Vatika	Camel's Back Road	2632628
Yashoda Bhavan	Spring Road	2630105
Spring Side Inn	Bhatta Village	9412050171
Bhandari Estate	Spring Road	2632339, 2631758
Baijnath Niwas	Gandhi Chowk	2630049
Jaiswal Estate	Kingreig Road	-
Vale View	Circular Road	2633275
Savitri Villa	Camel's Back Road	2632128
Madhu Rastogi, Creig Cottage	Near Hampton Court School	2631457
A.K. Mehendiratta	Camel's Back Road	2631090
'SAI' Paying Guest House	Mall Road	2631259
'City Castle'	Near Clock Tower	2631418, 2630162
Krishna Palace Guest House	Near Clock Tower	2631348
Rain Basera PGH	Near Darpan Hotel	-
Classic Palace	Kulri	2631653
Hilton Palace	Kulri	2631432
Kalpana Palace	Kulri	2631412

NAME	LOCATION	TELEPHONE
Natraj Palace	Kulri	2631653
Rockwood Cottage	Kulri	-
Terrace Cottage	Mullingar	2632123
All Seasons PGH	Kulri	2631372, 2632872
Four Seasons PGH	Kulri	2631672, 2632872
Babbar Paying Guest House	Library	-
Rawat Paying Guest House	Jhoolaghar	2631479
Shikhar Paying Guest House	Jhoolaghar	2632702
Avnel Cottage	Near 'Bata'	-
Rajni Paying Guest House	Near Vasu Cinema	2631084
Swastic Paying Guest House	Tehri Bus Stand	2631796
Ravindra PGH, Krishna Palace	Near Clock Tower	2632332
Kailash	Near Clock Tower	-
Wolfbern	Landour Cantt.	2631440
White House PGH	Barlowganj	2630072
Yashin PGH	Jama Masjid, Kulri	-
Juyal PGH	Near Sylverton Hotel, Kulri	2632312
Mehrotra PGH	Near Municipal Garden	2631478
S.G. Inn	Clock Tower	2631212
Rock Heaven	Camel's Back Road	-
Jeet Singh Talwar	Kempty Road	-

Notes

Notes